W9-AHN-200

Judicial Activism

Bulwark of Freedom
or
Precarious Security?

Christopher Wolfe
Marquette University

Brooks/Cole Publishing Company
Pacific Grove, California

This book is dedicated to my children
Julia, Jared, Rebecca, Thomas,
Stephen, Trevor, Patrice, Elena, Marisa,
and Alex.
Few men are as fortunate as I.

Brooks/Cole Publishing Company
A Division of Wadsworth, Inc.

Printed in the United States of America

10 9 8 7 6 5 4 3 2 1

Library of Congress Cataloging in Publication Data

Wolfe, Christopher.
    Judicial activism: bulwark of freedom or precarious security
  / Christopher Wolfe.
        p.   cm.
    Includes bibliographical references and index.
    ISBN 0-534-14868-9
    1. Judicial review—United States.   2. Political questions and judicial power—United States.   3. Judge-made law—United States.
I. Title.
KF4575.W648   1990
347' .012—dc20   90-43089
[342.712]   CIP

Sponsoring Editor: Cynthia C. Stormer
Editorial Assistant: Cathleen S. Collins
Production Editor: Linda Loba
Manuscript Editor: Robin Witkin
Permissions Editor: Carline Haga
Interior Design: Linda Loba
Cover Design: Vernon Boes
Printing and Binding: Malloy Lithographing

PREFACE

I wrote this book with two purposes in mind and there is some tension between them. My first purpose was to continue my scholarly work by participating in an on-going theoretical debate about the merits of judicial activism. In this respect, this book is a sequel to my earlier work *The Rise of Modern Judicial Review: From Constitutional Interpretation to Judge-Made Law*, published by Basic Books in 1986. In that book, I described the historical transformation of judicial review from an essentially interpretive power to a primarily legislative one. I also discussed some of the factors that made such a profound change possible. Although my attitude toward that change was pretty clear—I think it was unfortunate—and although I did touch on some defenses of contemporary judicial review, I did not concentrate on arguing the merits.

This book is an effort to take up the questions only touched upon in the earlier one. Its purpose is to set forth and evaluate the arguments for and against modern judicial review.[1]

This effort does not occur in a vacuum. In the late 1960s and early 1970s, convincing scholars to seriously consider the theoretical foundations of modern judicial review was difficult, either because such normative questions were regarded as unproductive or because the justification for judicial activism was regarded as so well established. That is no longer the case. There has been an abundance of scholarship on the question Alexander Bickel put so clearly in 1960 in *The Least Dangerous Branch:* Since *Marbury* v. *Madison* (1803) is so clearly outdated both empirically and normatively as the foundation for judicial review, what should take its place?[2] The late 1970s and 1980s have seen a proliferation of theories of judicial review and, in response to them, an effort to resurrect a more traditional understanding of the nature and scope of judicial review.[3] This book falls into the latter category.

My second purpose in writing this book is in no way inferior in importance to the first. It is to provide a relatively succinct statement of the major arguments on both sides of the judicial activism debate. No book currently provides the educated citizen with a good summary of the major arguments and counterarguments. I hope this book will fill the gap.

One possible approach to tackling this subject would have been to summarize the major theories of judicial review that appear in the voluminous literature on the subject. However, I chose to lay out the building blocks of the various theories and examine their basic components. This approach can make a valuable contribution to the public debate by explaining the foundations of the contending positions on this important public issue in a relatively accessible form—one that scholars and undergraduates can both appreciate.

The question, of course, is whether it is possible to combine these two purposes: to contribute to the scholarly debate without leaving the average reader confused, and to summarize and explain the major issues for the educated citizen without creating a rehash that would be of little interest to scholars. I hope that I have been successful.

Throughout this work, I have made a good-faith attempt to present both sides of the argument on judicial activism persuasively. My rationale for doing so is not original, but it is always worth restating. First, as John Stuart Mill argued in *On Liberty,* we are unlikely to develop our own thinking as well as we should unless we make a real effort to confront the other side in its strongest, most persuasive form.[4] Straw-man cases foster a kind of intellectual sloth that encourages us to be satisfied with superficial reasoning. Like Cicero, we must realize that our first task in presenting a case is to study the other side and to know it as well as its best proponents do.[5]

Second, what I say will not be very persuasive if I do not consider the strong arguments on the other side that will occur to an intelligent reader. In the short run failure to confront these arguments will irritate the intelligent reader, and in the long run facile arguments give way quickly when they confront the real opposing positions.

That is not to say that I will avoid taking a position. I am firmly convinced that judicial activism is an unfortunate phenomenon and that the United States would be better off without it. That will certainly become clear at some points in the discussion. Nonetheless, I have tried to state the opposing view fairly, even trenchantly.

The form of the book, which flows from the immediately preceding remarks, requires a few words of explanation, and perhaps of defense. It is basically a dialectic. Starting with the more obvious pros and cons, I work through the issues by giving arguments on one side, and then noting the counterarguments, and then the original side's response, and so on. This process may require some defense because it is a bit awkward. Readers must constantly hearken back to arguments made pages earlier, and those who are unfamiliar with the elements of the contemporary debate on judicial review may find it confusing at times. It also means that a nice, tidy organization of the book is impossible. The form of the book as a dialectic requires each section to be larger than the section it responds to, because I start with one argument, then give several counter arguments to it, and then several responses to each of those, and so on.

Despite these possible difficulties, the dialectic form is extremely valuable. Most important, it avoids the defect of "talking by each other" that characterizes most intellectual and political debates. People speak on each side of an issue by pointing out the virtues of their position and the vices of their opponents' position, but often they do not directly confront their opponents' arguments. Effective speakers and debaters can slip out of an awkward spot, throw red herrings into the argument, try to cover up or get away from the weaker points in their argument, and draw attention back to their strengths.

My intention in this book is to make each side in the debate over judicial activism directly confront the arguments of the opposing side, frankly acknowledging the weaknesses of the position that happens to correspond with my own and the strengths of the contrary position. I cannot honestly say that I have done this on the basis of a confidence unalloyed with doubt that "truth will prevail." The relative merits of different forms of judicial review may be one of those issues where there are abundant grounds for different prudential judgments and where the truth is more "slippery" because it concerns practical judgment about contingent realities. Although the arguments seem to me to point clearly in one direction, reasonable people whose intelligence and judgment I respect will arrive at different conclusions. In these cases the dialectic form of argument is invaluable, because it is an effective vehicle for bringing out the strengths and weaknesses of both sides.

At the same time, I hope that a clear-sighted view of those strengths and weaknesses will have a beneficial effect not only in the abstract intellectual sphere, but also on public policy. At the very least, this examination may inject more reason into public discourse and diminish the impact of rhetoric on both sides. But I also hope that it goes beyond this to encourage a greater skepticism about the merits of judicial activism in its various forms.

Acknowledgments are due to a number of people who have read the manuscript for this book and given me the benefit of their comments, especially Bill Gangi of St. John's University, Stan Brubaker of Colgate, Gerry Bradley of the University of Illinois Law School, and Dean Alfange of the University of Massachusetts at Amherst. Reading manuscripts is a thankless task, and I thank them for it anyway, and very deeply. They are, of course, absolved from any complicity in my views. I also wish to thank Leo

Wiegman, then of Dorsey Press, whose encouragement in the earlier stages was and is much appreciated, Cindy Stormer, my editor at Brooks/Cole; and the following reviewers: Dr. David Allen, Colorado State University; Dr. Craig Emmert, University of Alabama; Dr. Stephen Graham, University of Indianapolis; Dr. William P. McLauchlan, Purdue University; Dr. Susan Mezey, Loyola University-Chicago; Dr. Kenneth Nuger, San Jose State University; Dr. Michael Perry, Northwestern University; Dr. Elliot Slotnick, Ohio State University; and Dr. Harold Spaeth, Michigan University.

This book would not have been possible without the generous financial support of the Bradley Foundation, which, together with Marquette University's sabbatical program, gave me a year free of teaching duties in which to write. I am also very grateful for a summer grant from Marquette's Bradley Institute for the Study of Democracy and Public Values, which freed me from the necessity of summer teaching in order to put the book in its final shape.

Christopher Wolfe

ABOUT THE AUTHOR

Christopher Wolfe is an associate professor of political science at Marquette University in Milwaukee, Wisconsin. He graduated summa cum laude from Notre Dame in 1971 with a major in government and went on to study political philosophy at Boston College, receiving his Ph.D. in 1978. During his graduate studies, Dr. Wolfe "migrated" from political philosophy to American political thought and then to constitutional law. He taught at Assumption College from 1975 to 1978, moved to Marquette in 1978, and was promoted to associate professor in 1985.

Dr. Wolfe's main area of research and teaching is constitutional law and American political thought. He has written numerous articles and a book, *The Rise of Modern Judicial Review: From Constitutional Interpretation to Judge-Made Law* (New York: Basic Books, 1986), on these topics. Religion and politics, especially the relationship between religion and modern liberal political communities, is his secondary field of scholarly interest. Some of Dr. Wolfe's writings in this area are collected in *Essays on Faith and Liberal Democracy* (Lanham, Md.: University Press of America, 1987). He is currently working in the area of legal philosophy.

Dr. Wolfe also co-founded and is president of the American Public Philosophy Institute (1989).

CONTENTS

CHAPTER THREE
Judicial Review and Good Government   73

CHAPTER FOUR
Democracy and the Indirect Effects of Judicial Review   105

CHAPTER FIVE

Conclusion   119

Framing the Issue

T he subject of this book is the pros and cons of judicial activism or, more generally, modern judicial power, but one cannot immediately leap into the specific arguments that will be its major focus. Discussion of these questions requires a prior framework; that is, a definition of *judicial activism* and *judicial restraint.*

This introductory chapter approaches that issue in two very different ways. One way is drawn from an outline of the history of judicial review in America. However, this history differs from mainstream scholarship by rejecting the assumptions of *legal realism*, the view that judges exercise essentially legislative power and that to some extent interpretation is inevitably an exercise of judicial will rather than an enforcement of the will of the lawgiver. While the influence of legal realism on modern judicial practice cannot be denied, it seems equally undeniable that an earlier era of American judges operated on a different view of judging that distinguished judgment from will and interpretation from legislation. Whether the reader finds this account of different forms of judicial review convincing, it is important not

1

to simply assume that the traditional self-understanding of American judges (with its ideal of judicial objectivity) was simply a myth.

This history of judicial review gives rise to a definition of judicial activism that focuses on the relation between judicial review and the Constitution: Activism and restraint are functions of the extent to which judicial review can be fairly considered an enforcement of the will of the Constitution, without an infusion of the judge's own political beliefs or preferences. The other, more widely accepted definition of judicial activism turns more on the manner in which judges use what is conceded to be a quasilegislative power. Accepting for the sake of argument the basic points of legal realism, there is still room for enormous differences of opinion regarding the extent to which judges do rely, or ought to rely, on their own beliefs and preferences, and their perception of society's beliefs and preferences, in their decision making. Even if one considered judicial *interpretation* appropriately and inevitably a form of *lawmaking* power, for example, one might still be sensitive to the argument that it is "countermajoritarian" and therefore be concerned about defining limits to it. Activism or restraint are functions of how free or how limited judges are in the exercise of discretion. Advocates of judicial activism emphasize the judicial imperative to "do justice" and tend to downplay restraints on judicial power, whereas advocates of judicial restraint tend to emphasize the limits they think should be placed on judicial power in a democracy and try to restrict judicial discretion in various ways.

Although these two definitions of activism and restraint are quite different, together they can provide a useful framework for the book's debate. I will begin with a brief discussion of the second definition, since it is the more common approach to the subject today, and then turn to a longer discussion of the other, at once more traditional and more radical, approach.

DEFINING JUDICIAL ACTIVISM: SOME CONVENTIONAL GUIDELINES

In general, scholars of judicial power avoid an "essentialist" approach that sharply distinguishes between *interpretation* and *legislation*. They prefer an approach that emphasizes the *interconnection* of law and politics. All interpretation, on which judicial review is based, involves some measure of political *choice* between the competing principles reflected in different possible interpretations of the Constitution's general phrases. Activism and restraint, therefore, cannot be reduced to the simple idea that activist judges "make law" and restrained judges merely "interpret the Constitution." Inevitably, the differences between activism and restraint are more a question of degree than of kind.[1]

Most simply put, the basic tenet of judicial activism is that judges ought to decide cases, not avoid them, and thereby use their power broadly to further justice—that is, to protect human dignity—especially by expanding equality and personal liberty. Activist judges are committed to provide judicial remedies for a wide range of social wrongs and to use their power, especially the power to give content to general constitutional guarantees, to do so. This approach can be fleshed out in a series of corollaries:

- Judges should not be tied down, in constitutional interpretation, to the intention of the framers, understood either as an historical set of expectations or as a determinate meaning of the language. This kind of constraint is not possible, in any event, because a whole series of problems make it difficult to know the framers' intent with certainty:

    * Which "framers" are the reference point? the whole Constitutional Convention? its leading members? the members of the state ratifying conventions?
    * How are we to know their intent? Are Madison's notes comprehensive and unbiased? What about the absence of records of debate for about half the ratifying conventions?
    * How are we to get around the uncertainty inherent in the very attempt to interpret language? Isn't language relating to nontrivial matters typically unclear to some degree? Don't efforts to interpret broad documents necessarily involve the creation of some interpretive framework? Is it possible for us to keep our strongly held convictions from influencing our interpretation of ambiguous texts?

    Even if it is possible to have a general idea of the framers' intent, the process of applying these general principles to modern circumstances is so complex and uncertain that interpreters must necessarily import much that goes beyond original intent. While hardly anyone argues that we ought to ignore original intent altogether, what does create friction is the importance assigned to original intent vis-à-vis the other elements of the complex, multifaceted decision-making process. Activists tend to accord original intent comparatively less weight than other elements.

- Activists tend to place less emphasis on adhering inviolably to precedent, especially in constitutional matters. The only way to change precedents apart from the Supreme Court reversing itself is the cumbersome amendment process, and so more leeway for Court reversals of constitutional precedent is necessary. Precedent is still valued for the elements of certainty and uniformity that it fosters in the law, but the major part of these benefits can be obtained while still allowing the Court considerable flexibility in overruling outdated precedents.

- Activists tend to minimize procedural obstacles to obtaining important and necessary judicial decisions. The details of a particular case, after all, are useful primarily as a vehicle for obtaining an authoritative Supreme Court ruling on the meaning of important constitutional principles, and procedural obstacles often serve only to make the process longer, more expensive, and more uncertain. Therefore, doctrines that have traditionally been used to avoid deciding important constitutional issues should be downplayed. These doctrines include (1) standing (the need for a litigant with a major, direct personal stake in the outcome of the case); (2) the political questions doctrine (the deference of the Court without independent review, to the decisions of other branches in some areas); (3) ripeness and mootness (means of keeping the Court, from deciding questions before the issues have been fully fleshed out and when the case has already been resolved without the need for a Court decision); and (4) various procedural matters relating to federalism (the existence of independent state grounds or considerations of comity). Often with help from Congress, the Court can also broaden the scope of judicial power by making liberal decisions awarding attorneys' fees and finding private causes of action. Overall, the general principle is not to let procedural requirements get in the way of achieving substantive principles of justice.
- Activists display less deference to other political decision-makers, because they have a stronger sense of the judges' own democratic credentials and capacity and greater doubts about the other branches of government. When a *prima facie* case can be made that an individual's rights are being impinged on, the activist is likely to shift from the traditional strong presumption of the constitutionality of legislative and executive action to varying degrees of "strict scrutiny" that place the burden of proof on the government to justify its action. Thus rigorous scrutiny will also be more likely to occur if the challenged action was performed by a state legislature or by bureaucratic personnel such as an administrative agency or law enforcement offi-

cials, rather than by a coequal national branch of government such as Congress.

- Activists tend to deliver broader holdings and broader opinions. They are more inclined to seek broad constitutional grounds. If the Court's duty is to resolve doubts about individual rights and government power, why postpone the vindication of important principles of justice? And why leave other political actors more leeway to frustrate the constitutional requirements of justice? For example, why formulate a holding in terms of a defect in the process, thus avoiding a judgment on substantive issues, if even a correction of the process would only lead to another suit and a new substantive judgment striking down the same law? (Although using a narrower ground may be tactically superior if it will "stick," since the Court may not leave itself as vulnerable to effective criticism.)

- Activists uphold a broad scope for judicial remedial powers. Judges must not only be able to declare certain acts unconstitutional but also ensure that further action will acknowledge constitutional requirements, as, for example, when courts find that prison conditions violate the constitutional prohibition of cruel and unusual punishment. To secure justice in such cases, courts must be able to issue affirmative commands, retaining jurisdiction of cases alleging a policy or pattern of widespread constitutional violations and maintaining ongoing judicial supervision of efforts to remedy them.

It might be argued that all constitutional commentators can be placed somewhere along the spectrum from activism to restraint on each of these issues. Nor is it impossible to be at one end of the spectrum on one issue and at the other end on another. For example, a judge may be skeptical of original intent (and therefore on the activist end of that spectrum) while being attached to precedent (on the restraint side of that spectrum).

In the context of this modern attempt to describe judicial activism, perhaps no factor is more important than the judge's underlying attitude toward majority rule and the "political branches" (i.e., the legislative and executive). If a judge strongly believes in majority rule and the representativeness of the political branches, judicial restraint will usually be the result. If, however, the judge has a more skeptical attitude toward majority rule and/or the representativeness of the political branches, a greater openness to the possibility of judicial activism will result. The degree of activism is likely to be determined by the extent to which the skepticism extends to the question of judicial capacity or incapacity.

DEFINING JUDICIAL ACTIVISM:
AN ALTERNATIVE APPROACH

Now we will turn to another, quite different approach to the question of judicial activism. This approach is embedded in a controversial account of the history of judicial review. This history and its implications will be developed by trying to answer certain key questions: How did judicial review fit into the overall design of the Founding Fathers? What were the ends they sought to achieve and the mix of different means they employed to secure them? What was the specific role and character of judicial review in this scheme? How did judicial review change as the constitution of American government was modified (whether formally or informally) in the course of American history? If judicial review is not the same power it was in 1789, how has it evolved, and what new purposes or forms has it assumed? And finally, what implications does this history have for a definition of judicial activism?

The Original Design of the Constitution

The Founders of American government were basically democrats, if we understand by that phrase representative democracy or republicanism, not direct democracy. Generations of scholars have invested their efforts in asserting the contrary, but those efforts have been notably unpersuasive, although they have persuaded many.[2] The fundamental truth is that the Founders intended to establish a government that was ultimately subject to popular control.

The word *ultimately* in that last sentence, however, is a reminder that the framers were not absolute or ideological or unreflective democrats. Democracy for them was not the unquestioned dogma that it has become in modern American discourse. The Founders were sensitive to the fact that democracy was a political means, not the end in itself.

The goal of government, according to the Founders, was the protection of the rights of man. This was clearly stated in *the* founding document of America—the Declaration of Independence:

> We hold these truths to be self-evident, that all men are created equal, that they are endowed by their Creator with certain unalienable Rights, that among these are Life, Liberty and the pursuit of Happiness. That to secure these rights Governments are instituted

among Men, deriving their just powers from the consent of the governed . . . .

Forms of government were to be judged on the basis of how well they secured these rights. In principle, a nondemocratic form of government based on consent and committed to securing these inalienable rights would meet the requirements for legitimate government set forth in the Declaration. For example, some Founders admired the British form, a classic example of "mixed" government.

The American republic was an experiment. The Founders knew from their broad education, especially their study of the classics, and from their familiarity with modern history and politics that republics had not fared well historically and were not faring well in their day either. And the problems that republics had faced concerned not only self-preservation against external foes, but also domestic tranquility and justice.

The Founding Fathers had reason to believe, though, that they could construct a successful republic, and they were convinced that republicanism was the form of government best adapted to the "genius" of America. Their conviction was based partly on the long practical experience of American self-government, since the colonies had ruled themselves to a significant extent even during the long years they were nominally part of the British empire, and partly on their understanding of a "new science of politics," represented by political philosophers such as John Locke and Baron de Montesquieu, that seemed to have developed ways to make healthy republics possible.

The most important problems the Founders faced were summarized by James Madison, in *Federalist* No. 51:

> In framing a government which is to be administered by men over men, the great difficulty lies in this: You must first enable the government to controul the governed; and in the next place, oblige it to controul itself. A dependence on the people is no doubt the primary controul on the government; but experience has taught mankind the necessity of auxiliary precautions.[3]

The Founders Fathers were sensitive to both parts of the problem. Their experience during the Revolutionary War and under the Articles of Confederation had convinced them of the necessity of an energetic and stable government. After all, the whole purpose of civil society was to preserve the rights to life, liberty, and the pursuit of happiness that were so insecure in a state of nature, and a weak, erratic government could not effectively accomplish that task. But their experience with the British and with the new state governments, in addition to their study of history and politics, made the Founders equally sensitive to the need to restrain government, or better, to channel it safely toward protecting rights rather than endangering them.

The republican principle, as Madison indicated, went a long way toward protecting liberty, but it was by no means sufficient. "Auxiliary precautions" were necessary. As Alexis de Tocqueville put it later in *Democracy in America*:

> A majority taken collectively is only an individual, whose opinions, and frequently whose interests, are opposed to those of another individual, who is styled a minority. If it be admitted that a man possessing absolute power may misuse that power by wronging his adversaries, why should not a majority be liable to the same reproach? Men do not change their characters by uniting with one another; nor does their patience in the presence of obstacles increase with their strength. For my own part, I cannot believe it; the power to do everything, which I should refuse to one of my equals, I will never grant to any number of them.[4]

To what auxiliary precautions, then, did the framers look to ensure the security of their rights and ours? To prevent tyranny of the rulers over the ruled, the framers relied on the *separation of powers*," so contriving the interior structure of the government, as that its several constituent parts may, by their mutual relations, be the means of keeping each other in their proper places."[5] A series of checks and balances within a definite government structure was the key: "The great security against a gradual concentration of the several powers in the same department, consists in giving to those who administer each department, the necessary constitutional means, and personal motives, to resist encroachments of the others."[6]

But separation of powers could only accomplish so much. If the three branches of government were separate from one other, but each was still accountable to the people as a whole, the serious problem of "tyranny of the majority" remained. What would prevent one dominant segment of society from depriving weaker segments of their rights?

In *Federalist* No. 51 Madison argued that two approaches might be taken to deal with this perennial republican problem.

> There are but two methods of providing against this evil: the one by creating a will in the community independent of the majority—that is, of the society itself, the other by comprehending in the society so many separate descriptions of citizens as will render an

unjust combination of a majority of the whole very improbable, if not impracticable. The first method prevails in all governments possessing a hereditary or self-appointed authority. This, at best, is but a precarious security; because a power independent of the society may as well espouse the unjust views of the major, as the rightful interests of the minor party, and may possibly be turned against both parties. The second method will be exemplified in the federal republic of the United States. Whilst all authority in it will be derived from and dependent on the society, the society itself will be broken into so many parts, interests, and classes of citizens, that the rights of individuals or of the minority, will be in little danger from interested combinations of the majority.[7]

Madison presented these approaches as two *alternatives* partly for rhetorical reasons. The fact that the "extended republic" argument provides a "Republican remedy for the diseases most incident to Republican government" means that "there must be less pretext also, to provide for the security of [minorities], by introducing into the government a will not dependent on the [majority]; or in other words, a will independent of the society itself."[8] Thus, the Constitution can be defended as the best *republican* answer to the problem of majority tyranny, as opposed to mixed government, the other classic answer to that problem, with its partial reliance on the hereditary principle, as exemplified by the British government.

But the Constitution suggests that these alternatives are not so completely opposed. If the extended republic is implicit in our political arrangements, so is a diluted version of the theoretical alternative, in the form of constitutionalism, with a special role for the judiciary. The Constitution could not be consistent with its republican principles if it set up a "will independent of the society" (a monarch), but it did set up a branch that was subject to less direct popular control and was therefore in a better position to protect rights endangered by oppressive majorities. *Federalist* No. 78 says that courts of justice, staffed by judges nominated by the president with the advice and consent of the Senate and serving during good behavior, were expected to serve as "bulwarks of a limited constitution against legislative encroachments," especially through their exercise of the power of judicial review.[9] American constitutionalism, then, operates partly by setting up institutions that will check and balance each other in the ordinary, ongoing political process, and partly by entrusting another, "non-political" branch with the task of enforcing the commands of the Constitution by refusing to give effect to laws that violate it.[10]

From the beginning, judicial review has been an integral part of the American experiment to establish successful republican government; that is, government based on the principle of majority rule, acting to accomplish those purposes cited in the Declaration of Independence. But the nature and scope of the power of judicial review has also been a source of great controversy throughout our history as well, especially because of the tension between judicial review and majority rule. Although this tension has existed since the founding itself, it has taken on new meaning as the nature of judicial review has changed.

The Transformation of Judicial Review

Important as it is to understand the original design of the Constitution, it is no less important to understand how it has changed during the course of American history. To understand the different forms of judicial review that have been dominant in American history is to understand some of the major alternatives that we can choose from today, as we face the perennial question of what the role of judges, especially Supreme Court justices, ought to be. An examination of history might convince us that earlier forms of judicial review were left behind because they were no longer adequate for the circumstances or newer purposes of American government. Or, on the other hand, the study of history might raise the possibility of resurrecting earlier forms of judicial review that may be superior to present-day forms.

This section presents a brief outline of the history of judicial review, focusing on how the nature of judicial power has changed.[11] It will also explain why a discussion of the contemporary role of the judiciary can be formulated as a question of the pros and cons of "modern" judicial power or activism.

Traditional Judicial Review

The first, or "traditional," era of U.S. constitutional history ran from the founding until the end of the nineteenth century. The chief features of this era can be seen most clearly by examining its approach to constitutional interpretation and its manner of exercising judicial review.

Constitutional Interpretation. Two of the most striking facts about developing rules of interpretation during the founding were the absence of discussion about them and the apparent widespread agreement on them.[12] Constitutional interpretation was viewed as a special case of legal interpretation, which was simply a systematized set of commonsense rules for ascertaining the meaning of a document. Interpretation began by looking at the words of the document in their popular usage and interpreting them in light of their context. That context included the other words of the provision at issue and extended to the much broader context of the document as a whole, especially its structure and subject matter.

The intent of provisions was commonly ascertainable from the terms and structure of the document; that is, intent could be grasped by an analysis of the document itself. The document was assumed to be, not a mere grab bag of disparate provisions, but a coherent whole, with objects or purposes that could be inferred and in light of which it ought to be read. Extrinsic sources of intent—the historical circumstances of its writing, the debates in the Constitutional Convention or in Congress, the ratification debates, contemporary exposition of the document (in newspapers, books, public debates, etc.), and writers cited by its authors—were subordinate but admissible evidence as long as they were employed with considerable caution.[13] These sources were to be used to explain the text, not to modify it; they carried weight proportionate to the evidence that they represented the general understanding of the provision, rather than that of a person or group only; and their authority touched on the meaning of the provision and only indirectly on putative applications of it.

Let us take one brief example of traditional interpretation: Does the original Bill of Rights apply to the states as well as to the national government? The First Amendment refers specifically to Congress, but that does not settle the issue for the other amendments (II through VIII), which do not refer to any specific level of government. This led to an early court case in which a Baltimore wharf owner damaged by the city's action in changing the path of a river sued in court for just compensation under the terms of the Fifth Amendment. Chief Justice John Marshall employed a variety of arguments to show that the claim was insupportable. He appealed to the uncontradicted history of the origins of the Bill of Rights, which was based on proposals emerging from the state ratifying conventions that manifested great concern over the power of this new national government, not a fear of the states. The amendments were appended to a document that created the new national government (the states already existed by virtue of their own constitutions, for the most part) and therefore the limits on government contained in the amendments ought to be construed to apply to the government created by that document. Finally, a rule of construction on this point could be drawn from the document itself. Article I, section 8 dealt with the powers of Congress; section 9 contained limits on government power but in many cases did not specify a particular government; and section 10 contained limits that applied specifically to the states. Given this structure, it was safe to infer that section 9's limits referred to the national government.[14] But if Article I, section 9's limits apply only to the national government (although that is not always stated explicitly), then the presumption is strong that the similarly worded limits of the Bill of Rights apply only to the national government.

These rules of interpretation emerge from a study of the range of constitutional interpretation during the first years of American government, and not merely from judicial instances of it. In these early days, much of the outstanding debate over the meaning of the Constitution occurred within the Cabinet and Congress and in public discussions (e.g., the debates over the constitutionality of the national bank, removal power, and the Jay Treaty debate, and the controversy surrounding the Alien and Sedition Acts). While there was certainly a great deal of disagreement about important questions of constitutional interpretation, especially federalism and slavery, the more striking fact is that there was general agreement on *how* to go about interpreting the Constitution and what the rules of interpretation were. That agreement did not eliminate controversy, but it did limit it and provide generally accepted criteria for resolving such questions. The most fundamental shared assumption was that the Constitution had an ascertainable meaning given to it by its authors and that that meaning was the end or object of constitutional interpretation—it was authoritative.[15]

Judicial Review. The classic statements of the case for judicial review are *Federalist* No. 78 and *Marbury* v. *Madison* (1803). The first, and more important, argument presented in both statements flows from reasoning about the nature of a written constitution. A written constitution that contains limits on government must be regarded as superior to ordinary law, otherwise the limits are illusory. Laws contrary to the Constitution are therefore void. Because "[t]he interpretation of the laws is the proper and peculiar province of the courts" (*Federalist* No. 78), because "[i]t is emphatically, the province and duty of the judicial department, to say what the law is" (*Marbury* v. *Madison*), and because the Constitution is the fundamental law, judges must, in cases to which the Constitution applies, give preference to it over ordinary laws.[16]

This primary argument is supplemented by Chief Justice Marshall in *Marbury* with some textual observations. For example, the federal judicial power is extended by Article III to "Cases, in Law and Equity, arising under this Constitution," as well as under federal laws and treaties, which suggests that judges must look into the Constitution rather than confining themselves to the laws. The supreme law of the land, according to the Constitution, includes not merely federal laws in general, but those made "in pursuance of" the Constitution, suggesting that laws *not* made in pursuance thereof—laws incompatible with it in some way—are not really law but are null and void. (Marshall might also have added that the supremacy clause looked to "the judges in every state" for the enforcement of the supreme law, thereby confirming the more general reasoning about the special role of judges "to say what the law is.")

Although judicial review was supported by most of the Founders, it was not the unquestioned power it has become. Today there is controversy about the scope or use of the power, but hardly anyone denies the power itself. In the founding, on the other hand, there were substantial theoretical criticisms of judicial review and significant political action directed against it. Judicial review won out in this early debate, but it did so in a relatively moderate form.

The two major opposing positions in this debate were legislative supremacy and coordinate review. *Legislative supremacy*, defended most trenchantly by Pennsylvania Chief Justice John Gibson in his dissent in *Eakin* v. *Raub* (1825), was rooted deeply in the principle of republicanism. Why should judges claim this proud preeminence of being able to set aside the decisions of other branches? The ultimate source of political authority in our regime, he argued, is the people, and if any branch is to be supreme in interpreting the Constitution, it ought to be the legislature, the branch closest to the people. Judges should confine themselves to the interpretation of ordinary laws, not the fundamental political laws.[17]

Coordinate review (sometimes called departmental review) was based especially on the principle of separation of powers. Thomas Jefferson, among others, asked why determinations by judges should in any sense bind other branches in the performance of their duties. Judges were free to make their own determinations of constitutionality in cases before them, but the executive was free to act on the basis of his own views, as Jefferson did in using the pardoning power to free those jailed under the Alien and Sedition Acts. He strongly assailed the alleged supremacy of the judiciary in the interpretation of the Constitution.

Jefferson also had objections to judicial review that were rooted in federalism as well. He and his judicial allies such as Spencer Roane of Virginia objected to Supreme Court review of final state judgments, even in cases involving federal questions. On various occasions in early American history, Republicans in Congress tried to strip the Supreme Court of this power, and although they never succeeded, the threats were quite significant at times.[18]

A straightforward assertion of *judicial supremacy* (something never attempted) would probably not have won out in the early debate, but in a more moderate form judicial review did emerge victorious. The most important argument in defense of judicial review against the charge that it was undemocratic was that the power did not imply the supremacy of judicial will over the legislature but merely the precedence of the fundamental popular will over both. Judicial review simply gave effect to the will of the people contained in the Constitution over the more transient popular will represented by the legislature (and executive) at a given moment. Thus, the very nature of judicial review kept it quite limited. To the extent that it was undemocratic, that was accounted for primarily by the nation's commitment to the principle of constitutionalism, whereby present majorities are limited by earlier extraordinary majorities.

Early defenders of judicial review also pointed out the limits that flowed from the nature of judicial power. For example, in *Federalist* No. 81, Alexander Hamilton argued that the danger of judicial encroachments on legislative power was really "a phantom." Besides the most important external check—the impeachment power of Congress—as grounds for this assertion he gave these factors: (1) the general nature of judicial power, (2) the objects to which it relates, (3) the manner in which it is exercised, and (4) its comparative weakness and incapacity to support usurpation by force. The last point is obvious because judges ultimately depend on the executive to execute their decisions; however, the first three points are less obvious. They refer to the fact that judicial power consisted primarily of the power to decide individual cases in accordance with law; that is:

- Judges did not lay down general rules for society, as the legislature did.
- They did not initiate action but had to wait for litigants to bring cases, and so they received them "after the fact."
- They dealt only with a certain range of issues that were susceptible to being presented in the form of a case. Many issues were not eligible because they did not involve tangible rights of particular parties.
- The form of judicial commands in cases of judicial review was negative; that is, a command to stop doing something unconstitutional, not a command to do something affirmatively.

These facets of ordinary judicial power were significant limits on the scope of its "political" power of judicial review. This reflected the fact that judicial review was not an explicit independent judicial prerogative, but an implied power derived from its essential task of deciding cases according to law.

Moderate judicial review also acknowledged the republican principle underlying the case for legislative supremacy, in the form of a "rule of administration" known as *legislative deference*.[19] Judicial review was not to be exercised in doubtful cases. Only when clear incompatibility with the Constitution existed would the judges declare a law void. Of course, there were enough varying opinions about when a clear violation had occurred to give rise to sharp controversy over the role of the Court in American politics. (Chief Justice Marshall's opinions on the contract clause and the necessary and proper clause, for instance, were the object of considerable criticism, and the Court under his successor, Roger Taney, made the mistake of trying to resolve the slavery issue with the *Dred Scott* v. *Sanford* decision [1857].) Nonetheless, the scope of disagreement on constitutional issues was confined by the general agreement not to exercise judicial review in doubtful cases.

The basis for this rule of administration lay in the very grounds for judicial review. In this traditional era, the only justification for judicial review in a republican government was the fact that the judiciary was enforcing the Constitution rather than its own will. To the extent that there was doubt about whether the Constitution was incompatible with a challenged law, there was doubt as to the propriety of judicial review. Judicial review did not consist in *giving* meaning to provisions that were unclear, but rather in enforcing the meaning that could clearly be found in the Constitution.[20]

Moderate judicial review also bowed in the direction of separation of powers—the principle underlying coordinate review—in the form of the *political questions doctrine*. According to this doctrine, the Constitution reserved some questions for the political branches. For example, even when a case turned on the question of which government was the real government of a foreign nation, the judges would not make that decision independently but would accept the determination of the executive branch, which was given that responsibility under the Constitution. The most notable example of this doctrine in early constitutional law was the Court's decision, under the clause guaranteeing each state a republican form of government, that Congress had the constitutional authority to decide which was the legitimate government of a state.[21] Or, to take a modern example discussed at some length during the Watergate period: Even though there could be an "unconstitutional" impeachment (i.e., for something other than the constitutionally specified grounds of treason, bribery, or high crimes and misdemeanors), it is *solely* the task of the Congress (the House impeaching, the Senate trying the case) to make that determination, which would not be subject to judicial review.[22]

Finally, the authority of the Supreme Court to interpret the Constitution was more qualified in the traditional era than it has become. Classic defenses of judicial review, such as *Federalist* No. 78 and *Marbury* v. *Madison*, do imply that the Court's interpretation of the Constitution has a special authority; that is, it is not *just* for the purposes of deciding a given case.[23] But that authority is not supreme.

The best-known historical example is Abraham Lincoln's response to the *Dred Scott* case. By denying Congress's power to prohibit slavery in the territories, Chief Justice Roger Taney's decision struck at the heart of the Republican party's position on the issue, the raison d'être of the party, which was built on the notion that slavery violated the regime's most fundamental principles contained in the Declaration of Independence. Lincoln adopted a carefully nuanced position in dealing with the case. First, he noted that the decision itself was binding, but that there was a distinction between the decision and its weight as a precedent or as an authority for the actions of other branches of government. Second, he acknowledged that the Court's interpretation "when fully settled" controlled not only the immediate case but the "general policy of the country" as well. But, third, he asserted that under some circumstances, the Court's interpretation could not be considered settled or authoritative. He then spelled out some of the grounds that might undercut the authority of the Court's interpretation: a lack of unanimity in the Court, the use of clearly incorrect historical facts as premises, apparent partisanship, and a conflict between the decision and legal public expectation and the steady practice of different branches throughout history. Even where these problems existed, the decision might be settled by being affirmed and reaffirmed over a course of years. But to say that the Court's decision on a vital public issue in the context of a single case irrevocably fixes national policy would mean that "the people will have ceased to be their own rulers, having to that extent practically resigned the government into the hands of that eminent tribunal."[24] Thus, Lincoln argued, members of other branches of government need not feel bound by every Court decision; for example, legislators could feel free to pass another law prohibiting slavery in the territories, hoping (either with or without new appointments to the Court) to secure a reversal of the earlier decision in the event of new litigation.

These limits on judicial review should not obscure the fact that it was a very important power. I emphasize them because they help to clarify the nature of the power. However important it may have been in early American history, judicial review was a different, more limited kind of power than what it has become, and no discussion of the appropriate extent of judicial power (especially the Supreme Court's) can proceed well without recognizing this fact.

This view of the early history of judicial review does not generally prevail today. More common is the legal realist view that judges back then were pretty much the way judges are now; that is, the ultimate grounds for their constitutional interpretation, within certain unavoidable constraints, included their own political ideals and preferences, or (what traditionalists would not consider to be essentially different) their own conceptions of what is required by the nation's ideals. The history of judicial review is the history of courts confronting the central political problems of their day and working out their own syntheses between the Constitution, precedent, and some measure of their own political views.

There is no doubt truth in the proposition that all judges are eminently human, and that in some cases they fall short of the ideal enunciated by Chief Justice Marshall, that they are to apply the will of the law rather than their own wills.[25] But it is a mistake to focus on particular shortcomings vis-à-vis the ideal and to dismiss the ideal itself. The problem is quite similar to a perennial issue of philosophy: If man is defined as a rational animal, then there are no men, for no man is perfectly rational. The classic resolution is that the definition focuses on the "nature" of a thing, what it is when it is fully developed, even though many, or most, or even all of the particular individuals in the category may not ever be *perfectly* developed.

Some scholars would go so far as to say that early American constitutional interpretation did not merely fall short of the ideal in some cases, but consistently did something quite different. Whether consciously or not, the ideal was verbal camouflage for what was really going on. How could one argue, for example, that Marshall, that "old federalist war-horse," as even his admirer Henry Cabot Lodge called him, came down with a "Federalist" constitutional interpretation *apart from* his own Federalist convictions?

The answer is simple, if somewhat controversial. Marshall could do it because the Constitution was fundamentally a Federalist document. The crucial linchpin of most legal realist arguments is that the Constitution is a thing of wax, not just because of what judges do *to* it, but because of what it *is*. If the Constitution has no clear meaning, then any interpreter must proceed by reading something into it. The crucial assumption behind the traditional position was that the Constitution was a substantive, intelligible document: It had a meaning and that meaning could be known with some reasonable certainty.[26]

Whether an individual or court was or is right about the meaning of the Constitution is a question that cannot be dealt with abstractly. The Constitution and the particular interpretation offered must be examined. My argument about the traditional era is not that its judges and outstanding political figures were always, or even mostly, correct in their interpretations. It is that there were generally agreed-on rules of interpretation during that era, that these rules—properly employed (and there's the rub!)—are generally an adequate guide to the meaning of the document, that the constitutional debates of the era demonstrate that the rules can be used effectively to establish the meaning of the document, and that where fair interpretation does not yield a clear meaning of the document, a necessary condition for judicial review is absent.

The judicial review of that era is distinctive because subsequent eras saw the emergence of different ways of interpreting the Constitution: Above all, interpretation became a process of creating new meaning, rather than of ascertaining and enforcing an inherent constitutional meaning.

The Transitional Era

The first fundamental shift in the nature of judicial review came toward the end of the nineteenth century. As is usually the case with historical developments, however, it had its roots in earlier phenomena. While the mainstream form of judicial review in early American history was based on the incompatibility of a given act and the Constitution, another form, which may be called *natural justice judicial review,* existed as well. In a number of different cases, justices argued that laws would be void (and could be declared so by judges) on the grounds of their incompatibility with principles of natural justice, even apart from the provisions of the Constitution. This form of judicial review eventually died out, at least in its explicit form, largely because it raised the specter of judges voiding laws on the basis of their own *will* rather than on the basis of *judgment.*

But another form of judicial review grew out of the natural justice form that may be regarded as functionally equivalent to it. In some state courts before the Civil War, the due process clause (originally associated with certain legal procedures) was transformed into a guarantee of substantive rights, in particular a right against "arbitrary deprivation of life, liberty, and property." On the basis of this transformed due process clause, a movement developed, especially after the Civil War, to protect property and economic liberty (freedom of contract) from legislative acts (not only expropriation, but also regulations that had the effect of diminishing property rights or economic liberty).

Another key factor that enabled judicial power to expand was the adoption of the Fourteenth Amendment, whose first section prohibited states from abridging the privileges and immunities of U.S. citizens, depriving people of life, liberty, or property without due process of law, and denying people the equal protection of the laws. While the primary intent of this amendment was to make possible congressional legislation to protect the civil rights of newly freed slaves and their white supporters in the South, the language was not limited to race, and over time new and expansive meanings were attributed to it. Its due process clause, in particular, became an important "handle" for a broader federal oversight of state activity. Ironically, this oversight occurred less in the area of racial discrimination than in economic regulation.

By the end of the nineteenth century, the movement to expand property rights protection had become a dominant force on the Supreme Court. Between 1890 and 1937, the Court often used the due process clause to strike down economic regulation at both federal and state levels. Because the now-vague contours of the due process clause provided the judges with an opportunity to read their own economic philosophy into the Constitution, this form of judicial review can fairly be considered essentially a new form.

Probably the most famous of these cases was *Lochner* v. *New York* (1905). New York had passed a law prohibiting work in bakeries for more than sixty hours a week. The Court noted that this had the effect of limiting freedom of contract, which was protected by the Fourteenth Amendment due process clause, and therefore had to be justified by some legitimate aspect of the state police power (such as a health law, because bakers had a higher incidence of certain diseases due to their job). The Supreme Court rejected this argument on the grounds that all jobs have some unhealthy aspects and that bakers were not exceptional in this regard. The Court also rejected the idea that the New York law might be justified as a labor law to rectify what legislators judged to be an imbalance in bargaining power between employers and employees, because bakery employees were perfectly free not to take jobs they did not want.

Likewise, the Court struck down minimum-wage laws for women, laws prohibiting "yellow-dog contracts" (contracts that forbade union membership), various kinds of state price regulation, and many others.

During this same period, the Court, under the influence of the same laissez-faire economic philosophy, struck down many laws passed under the authority of Congress to regulate interstate commerce. Although this interpretation of the Constitution was a more plausible one that rested on the clearly implied distinction between interstate and intrastate commerce, with congressional power restricted to the former, it was still doubtful enough to violate traditional norms of legislative deference. Chief Justice Marshall, after all, had maintained that commerce "among the several states" was "that commerce which concerns more states than one." In the twentieth century economic conditions have made that a broad category indeed.

The transitional era reached a climax in the 1930s, when the Supreme Court struck down many parts of President Franklin Delano Roosevelt's popular New Deal. Roosevelt counterattacked with his Court-packing plan, and in the middle of that battle the Court switched its position.[27] After *National Labor Relations Board* v. *Jones-Laughlin Steel Corporation* in 1937, the Court consistently upheld economic regulation against challenges—based on both the due process and commerce clauses.

One distinctive feature of this first era of judicial activism was the justices' apparent conviction that they were merely carrying out their traditional task of enforcing the Constitution: According to the terms of *Federalist* No. 78, they were exercising "judgment" rather than "will." There was no trace of the argument that what the Court was doing was changing or modifying the Constitution in light of changing circumstances or the argument that the task of judges was fundamentally legislative.[28]

The irony is that the critics of the laissez-faire Court were the ones who, despite their apparently deferential stance toward legislative power, had adopted views that would ultimately lead to a more self-conscious theory of judicial activism.

The Modern Era

The roots of the modern era go back well into the transitional era. Throughout the laissez-faire Court period, the Court's decisions had been subject to persistent criticism, and the character of that criticism had crucial implications for the succeeding era.

Origins. One of the reasons the laissez-faire Court had been able to maintain a traditional theory of judicial review while departing from its practice was its understanding of the framers, property rights, and the Constitution. Late nineteenth-century admirers of the framers often played up the idea that the judiciary had been intended to be a bastion of property rights against the attempts of the democratic mob to plunder the propertied. (The kernel of truth in this was that the framers did expect the judiciary to prevent the violation of contractual rights through the constitutional provision that forbade states to impair the obligation of contracts. But this more focused protection of property rights was not equivalent to a due process clause which was virtually a blank check for the judges to strike down regulations of property they considered arbitrary.) Critics of the laissez-faire Court might have rejected this approach, citing evidence that the founding generation accepted with equanimity the idea that property rights were subject to a broad range of legislative regulations.[29] But instead, the critics accepted the assertion that the laissez-faire Court's actions more or less conformed to the Founders' desires and expectations. The point of their attack was not that the Court had departed from the original meaning of the Constitution, but rather that the meaning of the Constitution had to be understood in light of the new needs of an era whose circumstances could not have been foreseen by its framers. It had to be adapted to the times.

It is not surprising that the critics took this line. Late nineteenth-century thought was profoundly influenced by the impact of evolutionary thought. Charles Darwin was a major intellectual force. As Woodrow Wilson argued in his book *Constitutional Government in the United States*, the Constitution was made in light of a more Newtonian view of the world, but late nineteenth-century thinkers were more likely to see it in Darwinian terms.[30]

This emphasis on evolution was also a major factor in the developing view of judicial power. A crucial turning point in American thought was the publication in 1881 of *The Common Law* by Oliver Wendell Holmes, Jr. Holmes argued that prevailing views of the common law had not given an adequate account of its historical development. The life of the law had not been logic, he said in a famous epigram, but experience. The most crucial factor in the development of the law was considerations of social policy, that is, what was best for society. Judging was not distinct from legislation, but a different form of it, in the "interstices" of the law.[31]

This new, "legislative" conception of judicial power was explicitly held to apply to constitutional and statutory law, as well as to common law. While the former appear to be different at first glance, because they involve judicial interpretation of written documents rather than judicial decision in the absence of written law, that is misleading. The common law judge did not act in a vacuum but employed principles from earlier cases that were more or less applicable to the current case. Those precedents were then applied to the case at hand, taking into consideration appropriate differences. Holmes and his disciples argued that constitutions and statutes provided the principles to resolve cases, but the task of applying them to cases often involved as much indeterminacy as applying precedents did. Defining and applying the principles of written documents, then, involved legislation in the interstices of the law just as common law adjudication did. In fact, it could be argued that the very generality of constitutions made constitutional law an area of unusual indeterminacy, and therefore an area particularly in need of judicial legislation to "fill in the gaps" of the law.[32]

An example of the new approach was the area of economic regulation. The laissez-faire Court, its critics said, was guilty of "mechanical jurisprudence," thinking that the law—in this case, the due process and commerce clauses—contained within itself the set answer to all problems, good for all times and circumstances. In reality, they said, such majestic generalities had to be understood as dynamic rather than static principles, with full recognition of the need to adapt them to changing economic realities. In the free-for-all of nineteenth century individualism laissez-faire economic ideas had once been appropriate for the nation's economic life. But times had changed, with the development of more complex economic relations (e.g., the transformation of a largely agricultural economy through industrialization, the increasing economic interdependence that transcended state boundaries, the growth of large corporations, the elimination of the frontier as an economic outlet), and laissez-faire economic ideas had become fundamentally outdated. New policies—and new constitutional interpretations—were necessary for a new age.

Ironically, the initial impact of these ideas was a tendency to be more deferential to legislative judgments in matters such as economic regulation. The judges' job of adapting the Constitution meant that they should reinterpret the Constitution so that legislatures would have wider discretion in dealing with new problems. Laws providing for maximum hours and minimum wages, for example, which had been incompatible with older due process ideas of freedom of contract, ought to be accepted under the new dispensation. The switch of the Court in 1937, then, together with Roosevelt's subsequent appointment of justices committed to such judicial reform, was widely perceived as a blow against judicial activism.

A Portent of the Future. There were hints even earlier, however, that the result might be quite different. If Justice Holmes was generally a great apostle of legislative deference, there was an important exception—freedom of speech. Together with Justice Louis D. Brandeis, Holmes developed the *clear and present danger* test to evaluate what speech remained unprotected by the First Amendment. (After 1925, the Court held that the guarantee of free speech was applicable to the states under the Fourteenth Amendment.)

It seems obvious to contemporary Americans that the First Amendment was intended to provide broad protection for speech, subject only to the fact that some speech must necessarily be curtailed. Holmes's example was shouting "Fire!" in a crowded theater. Justices Hugo L. Black and William D. Douglas, among others, have argued that the amendment literally means what it says—that no speech may be suppressed. But the dominant position in early American life was that its meaning was another "literal" meaning, namely that *freedom* of speech, as distinct from *licentious* speech, was protected. In other words, an individual was free to speak (i.e., free from prior restraints), but he or she was subject to punishment, pursuant to law and trial by jury, if that power was abused in a way that was harmful to the community. This was basically the meaning of freedom of speech in English law at the time of the founding.

By the twentieth century, judges had confined the grounds for restricting speech to some relation between speech and illegal acts. If speech had a tendency to bring about illegal acts, then it could legitimately be prohibited. The Court espoused that position throughout the 1920s, as Justice Holmes and Brandeis developed their alternative position—the clear and present danger test—in dissents and concurrences.

The clear and present danger test treated the First Amendment as a strong, but not absolute, general presumption in favor of free speech. The circumstances under which speech could be curtailed were quite limited: There must be a serious evil that the legislature had a right to prohibit, and the danger must be imminent. The very requirement of such conditions suggested that the burden of proof rested on the government rather than on the defendant. One crucial element of the test was that the defendant could claim that no such danger existed in his or her case. That is, a legislative judgment that a certain *kind* of speech constituted a clear and present danger was inadequate; free speech was so important that it could be restricted only if it could be shown that it was necessary to do so *now* in *these* circumstances. This distinction was crucial because it suggested that *judges* would make the ultimate determination of what constituted a clear and present danger. In effect, judges would make the policy judgments on what speech should be protected and what should be subject to restriction in our society. This determination would clearly have been a legislative judgment under a more traditional approach, since it went beyond the guidance the Constitution provided in the matter. Modern exponents of free speech, however, are leery about entrusting such questions to legislatures, because they believe that legislatures are too willing to subordinate free speech values to other interests.

Under the new approach, judges are less concerned with *interpretation* in the strict sense of the term than with "specifying the application of vague constitutional generalities." Judges do not simply announce what the Constitution says about certain questions; rather they are delegated power to determine what policies will best effectuate the document's vague presumptions. This new, broader view of interpretation is defended as the best way to combine the principle of permanent constitutional principles and the reality of constant change.

Development on the Supreme Court. After 1937, the modern understanding of interpretation and judicial power became dominant on the Supreme Court. Not surprisingly, the first area in which the Court asserted its power, in a manner quite unlike its new deference in economic affairs, was the First Amendment. Starting in the late 1930s, and throughout the 1940s, the Court showed an increased sensitivity to free speech and religion claims. By the end of that period, it was possible to speak of the "preferred freedoms" of the First Amendment. Even Justice Felix Frankfurter, who protested against the tendency to regard any challenged legislation as "presumptively unconstitutional," noted that there was something special about freedom of speech. Speaking of Justice Holmes, Frankfurter said that since

> the progress of civilization is to a considerable extent the displacement of error which once held sway as official truth by beliefs which in turn have yielded to other beliefs, for him the right to search for truth was of a different order than some transient economic dogma. And without freedom of expression, thought becomes checked and atrophied. Therefore, in considering what interests are so fundamental as to be enshrined in the due process clause, those liberties of the individual which history has attested as the indispensable conditions of an open as against a closed society come to this Court with a momentum for respect lacking when appeal is made to liberties which derive merely from shifting economic arrangements.[33]

Some principles are so important to our political and social arrangements that the Court singles them out for special protection and downplays or even disregards the normal presumption of constitutionality with which it approaches legislation.

A crucial step in the expansion of judicial power in the modern era came in 1954 in *Brown* v. *Board of Education of Topeka*. After the Civil War, there had been some efforts to protect the rights of blacks in the South, but the North eventually withdrew, and slowly but surely a system of white supremacy was reestablished. By the beginning of the twentieth century, segregation enforced by law was the way of life in the South; this fact was also true to a considerable extent in the North, although less completely and not generally as a matter of law. The Supreme Court upheld segregation in *Plessy* v. *Ferguson* in 1896, arguing that "separate but equal" facilities were compatible with equal protection of the law. But separate invariably meant unequal, as southern blacks were reduced to an inferior caste.

Scattered efforts were made to improve race relations in the country through the twentieth century, but few had broad social ramifications. One set of efforts was the legal battles fought by the NAACP to obtain equal educational opportunity. A number of skirmishes were won before and after World War II, but by the early 1950s it was time to tackle (supposedly) "separate but equal" education head-on.

The Supreme Court took up the issue in *Brown* v. *Board of Education of Topeka*. After the initial argument, it asked for reargument on the question of the intention of the framers of the Fourteenth Amendment. Had they intended the guarantee of equal protection of the laws to include a prohibition of segregated education? The lawyers came back with their "law office history," each side having gathered whatever historical evidence supported its case, and the Supreme Court declared the contest a draw. The Court had to take that approach because it was intent on dismantling the unjust system of white supremacy, and the historical materials showed pretty clearly that the framers of the Fourteenth Amendment had not intended to prohibit segregated education. The Court went on to say that in its examination of public education and segregation, "we cannot turn the clock back to 1868 when the Amendment was adopted, or even to 1896 when *Plessy* v. *Ferguson* was written"[34] but must look at what public education had become.

Instead of relying on historical intent, the Court relied on social science evidence, which suggested that segregated education had a negative effect on the motivation of black students and therefore was inherently unequal. Whether that was so, and there were some sharp critiques of the Court's opinion, there was general support for the opinion in the North because, whatever the effect on students' motivation, segregation was seen as a system built on white supremacy. Whatever the more specific intentions of the framers of the Fourteenth Amendment, the feeling was that the moral impulse underlying the Civil War amendments called for a society based on racial equality, and that meant the end of legal segregation.

The Court's effort to bring about a massive social reform—the transformation of a whole way of life in an entire region of the nation—was successful, although it took some time to accomplish and ultimately relied on action in the ordinary political process, such as the Civil Rights Act of 1964 and the Voting Rights Act of 1965. Few people in contemporary society see the effect of *Brown* itself as anything other than a great triumph for justice. Rather than expending or depleting the Court's "capital," its institutional prestige, the case in the long run added to it considerably. *Brown* gave the Court confidence that it could indeed bring about important social reforms in a way that would be regarded as legitimate by most Americans. Such confidence was a great stimulus to expand Court power to achieve further social reform.

One important aspect of the way in which the Court handled school desegregation was the use of its *remedial power*. The Court did not simply say that henceforth school assignment would have to be done on a basis other than race. Its initial order gave some leeway for delay in light of administrative difficulty, and during this time the local courts supervising the desegregation retained jurisdiction over the case. Eventually, the Supreme Court ruled that the only satisfactory form of desegregation would substantially eliminate racial imbalance. Local courts were given broad discretion to determine what kinds of plans were necessary to accomplish this goal and often exercised detailed control over various school policies for extended periods. Rather than exercising a simple nay-saying power, then, courts began to issue many affirmative commands, specifying what school boards and others had to do. This expansion of the courts' equitable or remedial powers has played a substantial role in the expansion of contemporary judicial power.[35]

This is not the place to give a complete summary of what the modern Supreme Court has done with its expanded power. (Some of those cases will come out in the arguments in later chapters.) For the moment, it will have to be enough to say that the Court has generally been solicitous in expanding the protection of civil liberties and certain forms of equality. There have been ups and downs in this undertaking, especially under the Warren Court's successors, the Burger and Rehnquist Courts; but overall where the Court has changed the law, it has more often followed policies that are generally supported by liberals and opposed by conservatives. Although there are important recent exceptions in the fields of separation of powers, "takings" of property, and affirmative action, most of the cases about which liberals are unhappy involve the Court's refusal to mandate liberal policies rather than its promulgation of conservative ones.

Apart from the political consequences of Court decisions, however, it is important to look at the general character of modern constitutional interpretation and judicial review. In principle, after all, this same approach could be adapted to more conservative purposes, as the initial, laissez-faire form of modern judicial practice and some recent cases have shown.

Constitutional Interpretation. Modern constitutional interpretation is generally based on a reading of particular constitutional phrases as very broad general presumptions or guiding principles, as opposed to "absolutes" to be construed "literally." The difference between traditional and modern interpretation, then, begins with differences over the meaning of certain key phrases. Were they intended to have, or do they in fact have, some relatively determinate content that interpreters should focus on, or were they intended to be, or are they in fact, open-ended provisions whose content must be determined by courts over time?

The most important phrases have been the due process clauses of the Fifth and Fourteenth Amendments, the Fourteenth Amendment's equal protection clause, the guarantees of freedom of speech and religion in the First Amendment, and recently the Ninth Amendment.[36] Modern interpreters have given the due process clause a very broad meaning: It guarantees fundamental rights against arbitrary deprivation. However, the Constitution does not specify which rights are fundamental and what constitutes arbitrary deprivation; the judges must develop these answers by adjudication over time. Likewise, the equal protection clause guarantees against unreasonably unequal or different treatment; the standard formulation is that people situated similarly must be treated equally. The interpreter would have to specify what kinds of different treatment would be unreasonable.

The First Amendment guarantee of free speech establishes the principle that free speech is very important, and it requires state interests justifying restrictions on free speech to be very important ones. The guarantee of free exercise of religion means that religious belief cannot be mandated or prohibited and that religiously based action can be restricted only for very important state interests. (The clause forbidding laws respecting an establishment of religion is treated a bit differently; it is more often treated as an absolute in theory if not in practice. The differences in such cases shift to questions about the definition of *establishment*.)

The modern Court, and many of its supporters, tends to argue that key constitutional phrases were intended by their authors to be open-ended. In this sense, they can be viewed as delegating power to future interpreters to determine certain questions. Others would prescind from the issue of original intent and simply say that on face value the provisions are open-ended and that they are inevitably so, since any attempt to establish provisions with specific content would have been both impossible and undesirable.

Thus, the main job of interpretation in the modern era is not so much obtaining the meaning of the words of the Constitution—the general principles are relatively easy to establish—as applying those general meanings to particular cases to give them specific content in regard to the issues involved. This process may be characterized as a "balancing" process. In each case, judges must evaluate (1) the importance of the asserted right, especially in the form in which it is presented in the case; (2) the importance of the state interests said to justify impinging on that right; and (3) whether the state interests justify such impingement as the case involves. In some areas, modern judges engage in this process with a presumption in favor of the right (i.e., the burden of proof is on the government, at least after a prima facie showing that a constitutional right has been restricted in some way), although the frequency and extent of that presumption varies.

The content of the balancing process clearly reveals the similarity between the judges' new duties and what goes on in the normal legislative process or it might be argued, what would go on in the ordinary legislative process, if it chose to be more concerned about rights than it tends to be. It is not a question of simply applying a clear principle to facts that fall within the operation of that principle. Rather it is a question of defining or giving content to a vague principle in a case involving certain factual circumstances. This is what Holmes and others referred to as "legislating in the gaps of the law." The major considerations shaping a judge's decisions will be broad notions of what is good public policy—what is most consistent with a broad conception of the Constitution's general "ideals" (e.g., liberty, equality, human dignity).[37]

Features of Modern Judicial Review. The modern approach to constitutional interpretation and judicial review is a fundamental transformation of older notions; it is essentially a different power. Some implications of that transformation can be seen by comparing the corollaries of modern or "expansive" judicial review with the features of traditional or "moderate" judicial review.

Traditional judicial review tried to maintain its "democratic credentials" by arguing that judges were not enforcing their own wills, but simply the will of the people as contained in the Constitution. (If this was undemocratic, it was because at one point in history a popular majority—even though a special kind of popular majority acting in its "constitutive" capacity—had laid down the law that bound future, nonconstitutive majorities.) With the emergence of a new form of judicial review, which was more self-consciously legislative in character, that older defense was no longer available. As Alexander Bickel argued, after his critique and rejection of *Marbury* v. *Madison* in *The Least Dangerous Branch*, it was necessary to develop a new and more adequate theory of judicial review.[38]

Since the modern Court's conception of its power is less narrowly judicial, not suprisingly some of the inherent limits on judicial review that flowed from the nature of judicial power have been less important. The courts still do not explicitly issue "advisory opinions"—a constitutional opinion divorced from any case—but the "case and controversy" requirement has been diluted substantially.[39] This can be seen in the doctrine of *standing*. It is revealing that this doctrine, which requires an adversary relation between parties with concrete, nonnegligible personal interests at stake in order to constitute a case, was not formulated explicitly until the twentieth century. This was not because the nineteenth century did not adhere to the doctrine, but because it was so taken for granted, so unchallenged, that it did not need to be formulated explicitly. The need to develop the doctrine did not arise until constitutional law expanded dramatically during the transitional era, especially with economic substantive due process. Judicial review then took on a more "public law" orientation, in which the significance or centrality of deciding the conflict between the parties to the case faded into the background, and attention was increasingly focused on the lawmaking aspect of the case.[40] In this context, it is not surprising that standing requirements have sometimes been substantially modified during the modern era.[41] After all, if the Court has the fundamental responsibility to vindicate great constitutional principles of liberty and equality, then resolving issues without the delay and uncertainty due to legal technicalities makes considerable sense.

In this and other ways such as the expansion of class action suits and of declaratory judgments and liberal provisions for financing suits challenging government action, the modern Court, often with the support of Congress, has made access to the courts much easier and diminished traditional limitations on the reach of judicial power.

The principle of legislative deference has also been substantially modified in the development of American history. In the traditional era there were frequent complaints that courts had exceeded their legitimate powers, but there was also general agreement on the principle that laws should be struck down only when they clearly violated the Constitution. Twentieth-century jurisprudence is different because it is based on a theory of judicial review that cuts heavily into traditional presumptions of constitutionality.

For example, many contemporary theorists of judicial review argue—and the Court by and large acts on the basis of such views, even though it does not explicitly say so—that what they call *interpretivism* (interpreting the document, without any infusion of judicial will) is impossible because certain key, open-ended phrases (e.g., the due process clause, the equal protection clause, the privileges and immunities clause, the Ninth Amendment) are "quite broad invitations to import into the constitutional decision process considerations that will not be found in the language of the [Constitution] or the debates that led up to it."[42] Judicial review, according to these theorists, is a function of giving meaning to the *ambiguous* generalities of the Constitution. Ambiguity is the raison d'être of modern judicial review.

Modern justices have more explicitly rejected legislative deference in other ways. One early suggestion of this occurred in *the United States* v. *Carolene Products* (1938). Its famous footnote 4 suggested that "[t]here may be narrower scope for operation of the presumption of constitutionality" under certain circumstances—circumstances that have become the bulk of the Court's business: cases involving specific prohibitions of the Constitution (including the Bill of Rights as applied to the states), the "political processes which can ordinarily be expected to bring about the repeal of undesirable legislation," and the rights of "discrete and insular minorities" (e.g., religious, national, or racial). These kinds of circumstances seemed to call for a "more searching judicial inquiry" and "more exacting judicial scrutiny."[43]

That closer judicial look or "narrower scope for the presumption of constitutionality" turned out to be a presumption of unconstitutionality in many of the modern civil liberties cases that followed. Legislative deference was turned upside down as the Court placed the burden—often a heavy one—on government to justify its acts where, on their face, they impinged on a growing class of rights judged to be fundamental. This reflected the justices' growing conviction that the protection of fundamental rights had been entrusted to, and could only be adequately done by, the judiciary. The Court was not without respect for its coordinate branches (and, to a distinctly lesser extent, the political branches of state governments), but it became convinced that often minorities could only get a truly fair hearing in the courts. In general, legislatures are so taken up with the play of various powerful interests that they cannot be expected to be sufficiently attentive to the rights of those who are relatively powerless, which leaves a vacuum that calls for a special judicial role in protecting minority rights.

The political questions doctrine has also been subject to erosion in the modern era. Perhaps the single most important decision, although on its face related only indirectly to the doctrine, was *Baker* v. *Carr* (1962), which declared that legislative apportionment, challenged under the equal protection clause, was *not* a political question.[44] Earlier challenges to malapportionment had been made in the name of the republican guarantee clause of Article IV, and following nineteenth-century precedents, the Court had rejected them. *Baker* surveyed "political questions" and concluded that they were confined to separation of powers questions; since the case involved federalism—Tennessee's legislative apportionment was being attacked— that pretty much disposed of the political questions doctrine as a bar. Even in the separation of powers area the political questions doctrine is weaker today, as was demonstrated when the Court overruled the House of Representatives in its attempt to exclude a member, Adam Clayton Powell, in *Powell* v. *McCormack* (1969). [45]

That brings us to the last feature of traditional judicial review that has been modified, namely, the limits on the authority of the Supreme Court's interpretations of the Constitution. *Marbury* v. *Madison* actually said nothing specific about the general authority of the Court's constitutional interpretation; *Marbury's* intent was to show that the courts can refuse to give effect to unconstitutional laws in the process of performing their duties. Nonetheless, the reasoning suggested a certain preeminence of judicial construction of laws, with the Constitution being treated as one form of law: It is, after all, "emphatically the province and duty of the judicial department to say what the law is."[46] Thus Abraham Lincoln gave an accurate statement of the traditional approach to judicial review when he said that normally the Court's interpretation of the Constitution, when fully settled, is authoritative not only for given cases, but also as precedent for the future "general policy of the country." Lincoln did limit that power, however, in the name of the principle of republicanism; other branches could be justified by certain circumstances in not considering themselves bound by the Court's interpretation.

Chief Justice John Marshall was so successful in establishing judicial review that over time Americans began to identify the task of constitutional interpretation with the judiciary.[47] By the 1950s it was possible for the Court to say, in *Cooper* v. *Aaron*, that *Marbury* stood for the proposition that "the federal judiciary is supreme in the exposition of the law of the Constitution," and to imply that the oaths of state officials to uphold the Constitution were oaths to uphold the Court's interpretation of it.[48]

This kind of statement has been repeated on other significant occasions, such as *United States* v. *Nixon* (1974). These statements are judicial forms of a famous assertion once made (not from a Court bench) by Justice Charles Evans Hughes: "We are under the Constitution, but the Constitution is what the judges say it is."[49] Although Hughes supposedly came to regret that remark, that point of view seems widespread today. It is reflected, for example, in critical responses to legislative efforts to modify or restrict major controversial decisions of the modern Court (e.g., *Miranda* v. *Arizona* [1966], *Roe* v. *Wade* [1973]), and especially in the hostility that greeted Attorney General Edwin Meese's speech at Louisiana's Tulane University in 1986, which did little more than repeat Lincoln's position. Some of the roots of those responses were undoubtedly political, but they also reveal something about public discourse. In this case, they suggest that for many judicial review has become "judicial supremacy."

Defining Judicial Activism More Radically

This thumbnail sketch of the history of judicial review provides a framework for a sharper, more fundamental definition of judicial activism. Judicial activism, in this framework, is the exercise of "legislative" power by courts. That is, the pros and cons of judicial activism can be restated in broad terms as the debate between traditional and modern judicial review. Traditional judicial review—limited to enforcement of the clear commands of an intelligible Constitution—would represent the side of judicial restraint, while modern judicial review—based on judicial legislation in the "gaps" of a Constitution containing vague general commands—would represent the side of judicial activism. This is not the most widely accepted understanding of the term today, but it does have certain advantages. Above all, it recognizes that we are not talking simply about questions of degree but rather about two essentially different kinds of power.

Insofar as today's more conventional approach treats all judging as essentially legislative, it fails to consider a position that was dominant for the first century of American history. Thus, that method of defining activism rules out the most fundamental alternative to contemporary judicial activism. Now the modern position may be correct in arguing that the purported tie of traditional judges to the Constitution was specious, that they exercised as "legislative" a form of judicial power as modern judges. But it seems to me that the terms of the debate should not exclude from the beginning the possibility that the traditional approach might be a genuine alternative.

Moreover, using the tie between judicial review and the Constitution as the touchstone of how restrained or how activist judicial power is allows the inclusion of the second approach: Once modern judicial power is defined by its relative freedom from ties to the document, one can distinguish between different gradations of judicial activism by noting *how* freely a judge or commentator wants the discretion to be used. Thus, one can distinguish between more or less activist judges within the modern approach.

The major disadvantage of this approach is that it obscures another kind of activism, which is related less to the Constitution itself than to the manner of deciding cases and formulating opinions. These elements constitute prominent parts of today's formulations of judicial activism. For example, how far beyond what is minimally necessary to decide a given case does a judge go? How broad are the grounds chosen for the decision? How much discussion of matter beyond the immediate case is there? These kinds of activism could exist in the traditional era, and in this sense Chief Justice Marshall, for example, could certainly be considered an activist judge.

Given the terms of the debate on judicial review, however, it is even more essential to focus on the nature of judicial review, since the definition of judicial review vis-à-vis the Constitution is the most important determinant of the scope of judicial power. A judge who is very activist in the sense of John Marshall will still be substantially restrained by an orientation toward the Constitution. Even a modern judge who argues that judicial power ought to be used with caution because of its antimajoritarian character still retains the discretion to say that a given case is "important enough" to justify the exercise of very expansive judicial power.

For the purposes of this book, then, the terms *modern judicial power* and *judicial activism* are used more or less interchangeably. If in a given context I want to distinguish between them, I will do so explicitly.

CONCLUSION

Judicial activism may be defined in terms of either the relation of a judicial decision to the Constitution or the manner in which judges exercise what is conceded to be a broadly political, discretionary power. The definition on which I place the greater emphasis will be dissatisfying to most contemporary constitutional scholars, who subscribe to different conceptions of the nature of judicial power and of the evolution of judicial review in American history. For that reason, the arguments described in this book do not generally depend on adopting one definition of judicial activism or the other. Regardless of the definition adopted, the following arguments will be critical ones for evaluating judicial activism.

Some final caveats and qualifications. There is a certain artificiality in lining up activist arguments against restraint arguments. After all, even a given advocate of activism or restraint will pick and choose from among the kinds of arguments given here to produce a case for one position or the other. Nor is there only one generic activism argument or restraint argument: They come in all shapes and sizes. It is even difficult to use the image of a spectrum with people lined up along a line that ranges from "very activist" to "very restrained." Often a person's final position will be an attempt to delineate certain conditions under which activism is appropriate and others for which restraint is the proper approach, a "mixed position" of sorts. Ultimately, then, the reader will not necessarily be confronted with a simple either/or choice, even when the shape of the arguments seems to suggest that. At the same time, it is possible and worthwhile to describe and evaluate a general activist position and a general restraint position on each of a wide variety of arguments that are the "building blocks" of more complicated theories of judicial review.

One final qualification concerns the concentration of this book on judicial review and on Supreme Court cases. A complete examination of the issue of judicial activism would require much more attention to statutory interpretation and to lower federal courts. Generally, I have limited myself to Supreme Court cases involving judicial review partly to keep the book manageable in size and partly because most of what I say about Supreme Court judicial activism, defined in terms of the nature of judicial review, applies *mutando mutandis* to statutory interpretation and to lower federal and state courts.

CHAPTER ONE

The Constitution and the Need for Adaptation

IS THE CONSTITUTION INADEQUATE?

In the introduction I argued that modern judicial power is, and is recognized by many political figures and scholars as, a power to revise the Constitution, not merely to interpret it. One author described the Supreme Court as a kind of "continuing Constitutional Convention." Probably the most important argument put forward in favor of this transformation in judicial power is that so much time has passed since the Constitution was written that it is not possible for such a document to still provide an adequate framework for government in a society that is so different in many ways that the Founders could not have anticipated. Therefore, it is essential for some institution within our government to have the power to "adapt" the Constitution to our new circumstances; this is what judicial activism accomplishes.

Today everyone recognizes a certain limited adaptability within the Constitution itself, particularly in two respects. First, the language is very broad or general, so that it can apply to new circumstances. Congress can regulate "commerce," not merely stagecoaches; it is authorized to "raise an army," not merely buy muskets. Second, the necessary and proper clause gives Congress broad flexibility to choose whatever means are appropriate under given circumstances to attain the broad ends of the Constitution.

But the contention of advocates of judicial activism is that this flexibility is simply inadequate. First, even with this flexibility, the national government does not have adequate power under the original Constitution to meet important national needs, and therefore judges must be willing to add to or expand national powers by upholding and defending the use of new powers by the political branches. Second, the only way to guarantee that *limits* on federal and state government are "flexible" enough to apply to new forms of improper government restraints on liberty is to accord a kind of "necessary and proper" power to the judiciary; that is, a power to strike down actions that threaten to undermine the general purposes of constitutional limits.

The case for judicial activism is, in considerable measure, a case against the adequacy of the original Constitution ("fairly interpreted") for circumstances in twentieth-century America. If this inadequacy, including the inadequacy of the amendment process, can be shown, then some kind of "informal" amendment process is inevitable, and a major step toward the justification of judicial activism will have been taken.

The idea that the framers were limited in their ability to govern the future, even in the general terms they used in the Constitution, is not new. Powerful advocates of this view have been influential since the end of the nineteenth century. Their views are exemplified by outstanding justices such as Oliver Wendell Holmes, Jr., who argued in *Missouri* v. *Holland*:

> When we are dealing with words that also are a constituent act, like the Constitution of the United States, we must realize that they have called into life a being the development of which could not have been foreseen completely by the most gifted of its begetters. It was enough for them to realize or to hope that they had created an organism . . . The case before us must be considered in the light of our whole experience and not merely in that of what was said a hundred years ago.[1]

Or, as Chief Justice Charles Evans Hughes said in *Home Building and Loan* v. *Blaisdell*:

> If by the statement that what the Constitution meant at the time of its adoption it means today, it is intended to say that the great clauses of the Constitution must be confined to the interpretation which the framers, with the conditions and outlook of their time,

would have placed upon them, the statement carries its own refutation.[2]

Political life, like all life, is subject to change and evolution, and our constitutional development could have been restricted by "the too tight ligaments of a written fundamental law," as Woodrow Wilson, early in his academic career, thought it had been.[3] Eventually, however, he found an antidote to that disease in the judges' "statesmanship of adaptation."[4]

Implicit in this argument is the belief that, in important respects, the Founders' ideas and institutions are outdated. First, the Constitution was written before the "nationalization" of American life and thus concedes too much ultimate authority to the states and withholds too much from the national government, especially in economic affairs. Only by stretching the federal commerce power to the breaking point and beyond, far beyond what the framers intended, has the national government been able to deal with economic matters in a minimally adequate way.[5]

Second, the Constitution contains only a small number of limitations on the federal and state governments unless constitutional prohibitions are extended a good deal beyond the intent of the framers, as the Fourteenth Amendment and the Fifth Amendment due process clauses have been. The Constitution did not provide for federal supervision of the rights of state criminal defendants',[6] broad federal power to prohibit private racial discrimination,[7] discrimination on the grounds of gender[8] or wealth,[9] or broad judicial power to protect fundamental rights (e.g., the right to privacy).[10] Even rights that *were* protected, such as freedom of speech and religion, were understood much too narrowly.[11]

These problems reflect two kinds of limitations on the Founders. First, they were simply not in a position to foresee some developments, and therefore they could not provide for them. Second, their understanding of some of the principles they included in the document was inadequate because it was restricted by the limited perspective of their time.

The Limits of Foresight

Some of the inadequacies of the original Constitution stem from issues that simply did not exist in 1789 and that the Founders could not anticipate.

The Powers of the Federal Government. The issue of federal economic regulation is perhaps the most obvious example of a federal power limited by foresight. True, the Founders saw the need for the federal government to establish a framework for a national economy, especially by providing for a sound currency and eliminating state barriers to economic exchange. They also authorized federal regulation of interstate commerce in words that were broad enough to apply to planes and trains as well as to stagecoaches and wagons. Nonetheless, the provisions for federal economic regulation were too limited. Regulating "commerce among the several states," or interstate commerce, and by implication leaving intrastate commerce to state regulation, seems to have been seen primarily as a negative task: the prevention of discriminatory or "protectionist" state legislation. At that time economic enterprises were typically conducted within the state, and sometimes the resulting products entered the flow of trade leaving the state. Thus, the actual production of goods was a matter of state regulation; however, trade beyond the state again raised mostly negative questions of federal regulation, at least until the constitutional debate on internal improvements, such as roads, canals, and so on, began.

The American economy is now a vast national complex of many large corporations and smaller businesses that operate within their context. Not only trade—the movement and exchange of goods and services—but the whole process of production is part of a national economy. The Founders could not possibly have imagined the size and complexity of this economic system. Small Ohio farmers, who, in the nineteenth century, might well have shot any federal official who tried to tell them what and what not to plant, are now routinely subjected to the orders of the Secretary of Agriculture, pursuant to broad congressional legislation regulating the farm economy.[12]

It can be argued that the framers provided for federal regulation of commerce, and that, despite all the differences, that provision is still both present and adequate today—it simply allows for much more federal activity, given the expansion of interstate commerce. That is what the Court has argued since 1937, and perhaps it is true. But if so, can it be defended as a matter of original intent, given that the practical effect has been to transform the whole character of the U.S. government? In practice, the federal government is no longer a government of enumerated powers. Given the modern interpretation of the commerce clause (especially in conjunction with other clauses, such as the power to tax and spend money for the common defense and general welfare, as they are interpreted today), there is virtually no federal action that would be struck down on the grounds that the Constitution does *not* authorize it. The government may run up against certain prohibitions, such as the First or Fourteenth Amendment; but absent some constitutional restriction, it can do pretty much whatever ordinary politics permits. That is a profound change in the very nature of the American Constitution. If this change seems to be "authorized" by the commerce clause, that is accidental. The framers could not have known that someday there might be an incompatibility between two things they wanted: federal regulation of interstate commerce, and a federal government limited to enumerated and implied powers, rather than one possessing general power (i.e., the power to do whatever it thinks is in the public interest, absent a constitutional prohibition).

Limits on Government Power. Another example of the limits of foresight can be taken from the area of constitutional limitations, namely, criminal defendants' rights. Originally, in the Bill of Rights (mostly in Amendments IV through VIII) rights of this sort applied only to the federal government. At a time when state criminal justice systems barely existed, there was no need for federal courts to have the power to supervise them to prevent gross injustices. And had there been a need, the limited transportation and communication technology would have prevented efficient federal supervision.

Even more generally, one might connect the transformation of the federal government into a government of general power and the expansion of protection of certain liberties and say that because "big" government did not exist in earlier American history, there was no need for the kinds of checks on it provided by modern judicial activism. And perhaps the framers would have supported such judicial activism, had they been around to see the problems of big government that gave birth to it. In 1789, and throughout the nineteenth and into the twentieth century, the federal government's activity outside the area of foreign relations, including commerce, and war was minimal. Not surprisingly, the scope of judicial power was limited. The twentieth century saw a tremendous expansion in government powers and responsibilities, and perhaps it was inevitable that the restraints placed on government, especially in terms of demands for equal treatment, would also be expanded. The judiciary undertook the task of expanding these limits under the guise of their role of interpreting the Constitution. It may be more straightforward, however, to acknowledge that, just as the expansion of government power was quite beyond any intention of the Founders, so was the expansion of the limits on government.

The Limits of the Founders' Horizon

Modern critics argue that even apart from the inadequacies that resulted from the framers' limited foresight, the Constitution contains gaps that reflect the limits of their political philosophy. A brief look at several examples will demonstrate this.

Speech. Early Americans, including those who wrote and ratified the Constitution, thought that government stability was quite tenuous. This is hardly surprising since they had just survived a revolution, had experienced instability at the state level (e.g., Shay's Rebellion), continued to face hostility from powerful foreign nations, and were still experimenting with democratic forms (such as political parties, which were still suspect). Under these circumstances, the Founders considered government power to suppress seditious speech necessary, and this assumption shaped the early understanding of the First Amendment's freedom of speech clause.[13]

From our longer perspective, we can see that this assumption was unfortunate, because it provided those in power with an excuse to repress legitimate political opposition. The case of the Alien and Sedition Acts is a good example. Although bad laws, they were probably constitutional according to the original intent of the First Amendment. Time has shown, moreover, that the best way to defuse truly seditious activity is to allow a broad range of free speech. Should we, then, confine ourselves to the narrower free speech perspective of the Founders, or adapt their views in light of our experience?

Religion. The original Constitution, and the Fourteenth Amendment too, did not touch on questions of state religious establishments. Parochial religious views were powerful enough that about half the states still had religious establishments during the founding, and more progressive thinkers like Thomas Jefferson and James Madison (although able to eliminate the Virginia establishment) had to be content with a First Amendment that tolerated them.[14] Eventually, the more enlightened thought of the leading Founders spread, and state religious establishments were abolished within a generation or so, eliminating the contrast between state and national principle and practice in this area. Meanwhile, religious diversity greatly increased, and now even agnosticism and atheism, once subject to harsh social disapproval and sanctions, have been accepted as part of America's religious pluralism. Given this historical development, what would be appropriate? First, should we maintain a double standard for federal and state governments, which is the relic of a bygone age? Or should we accept a common national standard that reflects the broad social consensus that there ought to be a formal separation of church and state at all levels of government? And second, should we permit government support for religion and government discrimination against those who reject religion altogether, which accords with the original meaning of the religion clauses? Or should we demand that government refrain from supporting or opposing religion or any view about religion, including indifference or opposition?

Race. The area of racial equality presents perhaps the best example of the difficulties encountered with the Founders' views. Many opposed slavery in theory, but many fought to maintain it as well. Whatever the exact division, however, there was general recognition that slavery had to at least be tolerated.[15] Even the framers of the Fourteenth Amendment could only lead public opinion a certain distance toward protecting the rights of the newly freed blacks. For instance, at the time, the framers did not have the votes to guarantee blacks the right to vote, and generally they did not even have the desire to provide for broad social equality (including, among other things, the right to be educated in the same schools as whites where such public schools existed).[16] Most, probably, would not have accepted in principle that the black race was equal to the white race—except in that most important respect, natural rights. The struggle to achieve racial equality has been a long, slow one, and there is no reason either to ignore earlier contributions to that struggle or to pretend that those early contributors had an adequate understanding of the principle of racial equality and its implications. A more complete acceptance of racial equality had to wait for the efforts of the modern civil rights revolution. In light of this history, should the Constitution be confined to the limited views of 1789? or 1866? Or should it be brought into the twentieth century?

Other obvious examples of the Founders' limited political philosophy abound, such as the role of women in our society and the expansion of the boundaries that protect people's private lives and intimate decisions from governmental interference. These areas demonstrate that the Founders brought certain restricted outlooks from their own time and age to their constitutional efforts. If these views were to be regarded as authoritative, they would be an unfortunate shackle. Fortunately, it is neither necessary to feel bound by those outlooks nor to discard the Constitution completely. It is possible to maintain a firm commitment to the core principles of the Constitution—freedom of speech, religious freedom, racial justice, and so on— while adapting them in light of the progress of our national views over the course of history. Adaptation, then, is a key to sound constitutional interpretation; without it, the Constitution would be hopelessly outdated.

The Shortcomings of the Amendment Process

The inadequacy of the framers' ideas and institutions would not be as serious a problem if they had provided a usable amending process. What they provided, however, was hopelessly "cumbersome" and inadequate.[17] By requiring a two-thirds vote in each branch of Congress and ratification by three-fourths of the state legislatures, the framers made the amendment process almost impossible to use.

Major constitutional changes are likely to affect adversely some of the multiplicity of interests and opinions in society. However, by garnering the support of either one-third (plus one vote) of either branch of Congress or majorities (or at least blocking minorities) in thirteen states, an affected group can stop the process. It is not surprising, then, that only sixteen amendments have been passed in the two hundred years since the Bill of Rights was added to the original Constitution. That is an average of one every dozen years or so, although in actuality they have tended to come in clusters. Thus, many important matters have been left to "informal" amendment. For example, our whole system of electing a president has been so transformed by the emergence of political parties that it bears little resemblance to what the framers thought they were providing.[18]

The scope of national power would amaze the farmers and townsfolk who provided most of the votes for and against the Constitution. Government once had little or no direct daily contact with the average citizen, confining its attention to broad national matters such as foreign affairs and foreign commerce. Indeed, for the first century and more of American history, the post office was probably the major way in which the federal government touched the people. No amendment to the Constitution was ever passed to make possible today's broad-ranging, activist government, and it is uncertain whether such amendments could have been passed. Congress simply expanded its constitutional boundaries by passing new laws, which were eventually supported by expanded judicial interpretations.[19] Given the unwieldy amendment process, wasn't this inevitable?

Thus, the "time-bound" character of the Constitution requires that it be regularly adapted to bring it up-to-date. Simply to maintain the Constitution as it was written, even with the amendments it has been possible to obtain, would be an exercise in anachronism.

THE NEED FOR ADAPTATION: THE RESPONSE

In dealing with this argument, modern readers must first clear their heads of any unreflective assumptions of the superiority of their ideas and practices to those of the Founders. Our nation may be superior in many ways to the

America of 1787, but it may conceivably be worse in some ways too. It takes an argument to show why the Founders' ideas and institutions are outdated. The simple fact that our technology is so much more advanced is no guarantee that our political ideas are. That is true even if we have made advances in some respects; racial equality is the obvious example, although that has been more a working-out of what the framers hoped for than an alteration in goals.[20] In other respects we may be worse off. The point is simply that one would have to look at specifics to come to the judgment that change is necessary. Vague generalities about living in new circumstances are not enough.

The case against judicial activism must rest ultimately on a defense of the Constitution, including both its provisions in general *and* its provisions for change. Although some opposition to a revisory judicial power comes from "positivist majoritarians," who will accept whatever the majority wants and therefore do not like the idea of an antimajoritarian judicial check, the most substantial opposition comes from those who respect the political philosophy of the founding and the institutions created in light of it.[21]

The Powers of the Federal Government. Are the Founders' ideas and institutions outdated? Probably the most forceful charge, and one of the least debated today, is that the Constitution did not accord sufficient power to the national government in economic affairs, such as regulation of commerce and expenditures for the general welfare. Since the founding, there has been a "nationalization" of American political life, and the commerce and general welfare clauses have been interpreted in rather dubious ways to provide an adequate basis for the expansion of national power. The matter is quiescent now, basically settled in 1937 when the judiciary in effect ratified the New Deal, which is sometimes considered tantamount to an informal amendment.[22] Accepting this contention about the New Deal for the sake of argument, one might still argue that a formal amendment would have been the wiser path to take.

Why would a formal amendment be better than an informal amendment, which has been "passed" by Congress and the president and "ratified" by the Supreme Court? One very important reason is that a formal amendment could authorize additional national power without abandoning the attempt to limit it, as the Court has virtually done.[23]

It is one thing to argue that constitutional principles ought to be modified and another to say that they ought to be ignored. If there is a genuine consensus that the original Constitution did not adequately provide for the power of the federal government, change might certainly be appropriate. But there are very different types of change. For example, the Court could simply abdicate review in this area, permitting the legislature to do as it sees fit. This leaves the legislature free of any guiding and limiting constitutional *principles*. But popular support for ad hoc legislative judgments on particular laws that go beyond former constitutional limits cannot be automatically translated as a desire to eliminate the limits altogether. The alternative is to change the Constitution formally, thus forcing Americans to think through the consequences of the change and perhaps choose either to increase the federal government's power partially or to increase it broadly with some other institutional check on its exercise.[24]

The Limits on Government. But what about other matters, such as the absence of a greater number of limits on both federal and state government? Especially in light of the tremendous growth in government power and influence in national life, aren't the limits contained in the original Constitution (and amendments) rather sparse?

A good part of one's response to this argument depends on how one views the framers' attachment to federalism (and I am speaking of the framers as a whole, rather than only of Alexander Hamilton and the early James Madison, who were more nationalist in their orientation than most). To the extent that decentralization is desirable, the absence of more limits on state governments in the Constitution is proper, since every limit, in effect, "nationalizes" the particular political issue involved; that is, the Supreme Court, a branch of the national government, becomes the ultimate arbiter of the issue. Leaving limits out of the Constitution does not mean that state governments can function without restraint, but rather that the limits will be determined largely at the state level by the state constitutions (although sometimes by federal law as well). From this perspective, the absence of federal constitutional review of state criminal defendants' rights, of federal power to correct certain kinds of discrimination, even of federal review power in First Amendment issues, was not a constitutional defect but a strength. Some scholars would say that diversity of state policy in such matters, which can be complex or unclear (e.g., where does one draw the line on regulation of pornography?) is desirable.[25]

It is important to realize the difference between the two kinds of arguments on adaptation. The first argument was made by those who were unhappy with the early 1930s Supreme Court, which struck down much of the New Deal. They could plausibly argue that the original Constitution was written for an era that required a less active government; therefore, updating the document in effect meant expanding its powers, especially the power to regulate economic affairs. This was not just a question of the federal government's *lacking* the power to deal with those issues. The constitutional provisions for federalism, represented especially by the Tenth Amendment, erected a positive constitutional *barrier* to federal action.

The second form of the argument is more characteristic of today's advocates of judicial activism, and its roots are quite different. The claim is not that the framers failed to provide for sufficient legislative power, but rather that they did not limit that power sufficiently. For example, there was no constitutional barrier that dealt with the new technological problem of electronic eavesdropping. Although to some extent this problem has been dealt with as a matter of Fourth Amendment rights against unreasonable searches and seizures, it still involves issues that are quite different in important respects from those the framers had in mind. The problem was not that the legislature was shackled by the Constitution, modern libertarians urge, but that it was *not* shackled. The Fourth Amendment deals with similar issues, but it must be expanded (de facto if not de jure) to handle new problems the framers could not have foreseen, such as searches and seizures that do not require, thanks to modern technology, any actual intrusion onto property. This kind of case for judicial adaptation cannot be based on the argument that a cumbersome amendment process is obstructing a genuine national majority from realizing its reasonable goals, as Franklin D. Roosevelt argued. The argument here is against *both* a cumbersome amendment process *and* a majoritarian process too free to deal with the issue.

Even if the adequacy of the Constitution's particular provisions is seriously questionable (and I will take up some of those arguments later in evaluating the "good results" of judicial activism), that still leaves the broader question of the adequacy of its provisions for change. First, there is the legislative power, which is the ordinary method of change in American political life and which permits adaptation to new circumstances.[26] Legislative power is broad in scope, and there is wide discretion in the choice of means to implement it. When they wrote the Constitution, the framers certainly had in mind some of the problems that they faced, but they were even more concerned about constructing a long-lived government that would be able to handle whatever problems might arise. They considered the broad ends or purposes of government—especially the protection of inalienable rights such as life, liberty, and pursuit of happiness—to be permanent, but they realized that threats to those rights would assume many different, unforeseeable forms and that the government would have to be given broad powers to deal with them. Their primary goal, then, was a well-constructed political process. In many cases where it might be objected that the framers did not provide for a problem, their response would probably be "We did not provide specifically for it, but we provided a political process that could handle it."

Second, amendment power is available for those occasions when modification of the Constitution is necessary. Clearly, the amendment power is not an easy one to employ successfully. It was not meant to be used frequently. (Thomas Jefferson disagreed, but in *Federalist* No. 49, James Madison makes persuasive arguments against frequent constitutional revision, including the tendency to undermine attachment to the form of government and to rouse public passions, and the likely domination by the political forces most in need of being constrained. If the purpose of a constitution is to check certain actions by majorities, then the amendment process should not be too easy to use. Otherwise, such majorities could simply use a quick amendment process to do away with limits on their actions.

On the whole, however, the cumbersomeness of the amendment process seems to have been exaggerated. As Martin Diamond pointed out in his criticism of "scare arithmetic,"[27] not only can a small minority block amendments (i.e., bare majorities in the thirteen least populous states), but a minority can also pass an amendment (bare majorities in the thirty-eight least populous states). A more realistic appraisal of what the process requires would conclude that amendments can be passed if they have an enduring, nationally distributed majority. As much as any other reason, this explains the death of the sexual equality amendment; its supporters made no significant dent in the South.

Two reasons account for the small number of amendments. First, judicial amendment has removed the incentive for formal amendment in some instances. For example, only a few states must ratify a child labor amendment for it to become part of the Constitution. This step is unnecessary, however, since the Supreme Court long ago overruled the activist Court decisions the amendment was intended to overturn. We can only speculate about how many more formal amendments would have been ratified in the absence of modification of the Constitution either directly by the judges or through legislation passed by the political branches and upheld by the judges.

Second, it is difficult to put together a broad coalition to change the fundamental law of our nation, because usually a genuine national consensus about how to do it does not exist. Even when there is a broad consensus that *something* should be done, there is rarely agreement on *what* ought to be done. Thus, the small number of amendments indicates that there have been few occasions on which serious agreement has been reached on what changes should be effected.

This difficulty in obtaining the necessary national consensus may seem at first to be a reason to rely on an easier method of changing the Constitution. In fact, however, this is precisely the reason not to opt for an "easier" method that would give this power to change the fundamental law to something short of a national consensus—to a temporary or transient majority, or even to a minority. There is no question that judicial amendment is easier. Getting five people not subject to reelection to agree to do something will always be easier than persuading a national legislature and most state legislatures. But this ease carries a threat of tyranny; that is, unjust action that is contrary to the rights of Americans, majorities and minorities alike.

Moreover, the dangers of informal amendment, or de facto revision of the Constitution, are considerable. Above all, ready recurrence to informal amendment undermines the Constitution's permanence, making it easier to justify further modifications. This sounds attractive if the amending is being done by a group that one feels ideological fraternity with, but there is always the possibility that the situation might be different. Some of the advocates of judicial activism during the Warren Court years were considerably sobered by the new lineup of the Supreme Court in the 1970s and 1980s.[28]

Even if we concluded that it is necessary to amend the Constitution informally, the question would remain who should do it. The obvious first claimant to such a power would be the ordinary political process: Congress and the president. That would clearly be the closest majoritarian parallel to the structure of the Article V amending provision. Congress has in fact exercised such a power; most obviously, some scholars would argue, in passing the more constitutionally questionable parts of the New Deal.

The judiciary would seem to have a rather weak claim, given its not particularly democratic structure. If the objection to the amending process is fundamentally a majoritarian argument—that a majority is hindered from carrying out its will by the too restrictive requirement of an extraordinary majority for amendment—then why prefer the potentially "minoritarian" judicial process to the ordinary political process?

But now we are touching on the next round of argument: the relative status of the different branches of government according to fundamental democratic principles. And we will leave that for Chapter 2.

CHAPTER TWO

Judicial Review and Democracy

A s many of the best political and legal commentators supporting modern judicial power (e.g., Alexander Bickel, John Hart Ely, Jesse Choper)[1] have made clear, one of the basic starting points in the debate on judicial power in a democratic society is the anti-majoritarian character of the judiciary. The factors are easy to list: The Supreme Court is made up of only nine people; justices are appointed, rather than elected; and their tenure is virtually for life (i.e., during good behavior). Moreover, the nature of the modern Court's task is not to represent interests or to reflect the will of the people but to decide cases according to a law that is very flexible or malleable in its hands. Whatever the nondemocratic elements of other branches of government—and they are important—the judiciary is far and away the least democratic branch.[2]

One Possible (but Atypical) Response

There are various responses to this criticism of the Court as nondemocratic. One possible approach would be to concede that it is and to argue that this is consistent with the intentions of the framers. The Founders did not seek to establish a pure democracy, but rather a "balanced republic." They believed that democracy, like other forms of government, is subject to its own peculiar vices, and that these vices can be offset by incorporating certain nondemocratic elements into an ultimately republican regime. One of these elements is judicial review, which was established primarily to protect the rights of minorities against majoritarian tyranny.[3]

It is not surprising, however, that this defense of the Court is rare today. For one thing, it involves a return to the intention of the framers, and advocates of judicial activism tend to shy away from close reliance on those intentions. Their perspective tends to point out the limitations of the Founders' foresight and to expand constitutional interpretation beyond original intent, since that standard would sharply limit the Court's power to accomplish certain goals (especially *expanded* protection of liberty and equality).

The framers did intend judges to serve as a check on democratic majorities, and they certainly knew that judges constituted a less democratic force in our political system, responsive to law rather than to immediate popular will. But as far as judicial review was concerned, the judges' power was to enforce a democratic Constitution, not some other perception of what principles would be best for the nation.[4] The founding generation distrusted political power that was not sufficiently limited, and the dearth of checks on the judiciary is a testimony to their limited conception of judicial power. Even the draconian character of such checks as impeachment suggests that the Founders viewed them as last resorts in extreme cases rather than as a regular part of the give-and-take mechanism of the separation of powers.

With respect to the protection of minority rights, the framers rejected the idea of relying on a will independent of society, as James Madison said in *Federalist* No. 51.[5] Further, there is little evidence that they placed their primary reliance on a judiciary that was substantially independent of popular control for long periods, much less a judiciary whose power was to be exercised independently from the Constitution. Rather, their chief reliance was on the extended republic argument of *Federalist* No. 10, which held that a large republic had two advantages. First, it would have a larger pool from which to choose representatives and, therefore, would be likely to obtain better people to "refine and enlarge" public opinion. Moreover, the larger electorate would make it harder to successfully practice "vicious arts" in elections. Second, an extended republic would include a great multiplicity of interests, making it unlikely that any homogeneous group could impose its desires on society. Majorities could be formed only by a process of compromise and coalition among the many groups—a process that would tend to produce moderate majorities.[6] In addition, the Founders relied heavily on federalism and on a separation of powers that focused on mutual checks between the legislature and the executive.[7]

Defenders of judicial activism also do not typically rely on the framers' intentions because one purpose of judicial activism is to "interpret" the Constitution in ways that go beyond or even against what the framers intended. Modern activist decisions are much more libertarian and egalitarian than the views of the Founders, as Leonard Levy and Walter Berns have shown with regard to freedom of speech, and Raoul Berger has shown with respect to the Fourteenth Amendment.[8]

The greater libertarianism and egalitarianism of contemporary proponents of judicial activism also suggests that they tend to be uncomfortable relying on an argument that judicial review is undemocratic and that it ought to be that way. In general, they are strongly committed ideologically to democracy and would argue that their goal is to make the nation more democratic.

THE DEMOCRATIC CHARACTER OF JUDICIAL ACTIVISM

The more typical response to the charge that judicial activism is undemocratic is to contest the issue of the Court's nondemocratic character. There are three major arguments in response to that charge: (1) the essential purposes of the Court are vitally democratic, (2) judges are ultimately subject to popular control, and (3) modern judicial power has been legitimized by tacit consent.

The Democratic Purposes of Judicial Review

Judicial activism claims to have distinctively democratic purposes, namely the protection of liberty and the expansion of equality. It is not a new observation that democracy has certain ends that it values. Aristotle defined regimes by asking not only about who rules (the organization of offices and the source of political power), but also about the ends of the regime (its typical goals or purposes). In discussing the principles of democracy, he noted that "the basis of a democratic state is liberty; which, according to the common opinion of men, can only be enjoyed in such a state;—this they affirm to be the great end of every democracy." One aspect of liberty is majority rule, and "another is that a man should live as he likes."[9]

Aristotle's observation seems to be confirmed in the American setting by the Declaration of Independence, which holds that the purpose of government is to protect man's inalienable rights, such as life, liberty, and the pursuit of happiness.[10] Whatever the status of judicial review in a pure majoritarian regime, it fits very well into a scheme of liberal democracy, which is the American understanding of democracy.[11]

The most frequently cited expression of this argument is the *Carolene Products* footnote, which provides a rationale for an expanded judicial role in the protection of liberty.[12] Justice Harlan Stone argued that the normal presumption of constitutionality with which judges approach the review of legislation has less justification if laws (1) fall within the sphere of specific constitutional rights (the Fourteenth Amendment due process clause being considered specific insofar as it applies Bill of Rights guarantees to the states), (2) impinge in some way on the integrity of the political process (e.g., voting rights, freedom of speech), or (3) are directed against discrete and insular minorities (e.g., racial and religious minorities). Why did he choose these three cases?

Specific constitutional rights, such as freedom of speech and religion or freedom from self-incrimination, give greater direction to judges and provide a more explicit presumption in favor of a particular constitutional "value" than do the vague confines of the due process or equal protection clauses. This specificity gives judges greater leeway for a "more searching judicial inquiry."[13]

But the special necessity for the judiciary to become more involved stands out more in the second and third parts of the footnote. Political rights are a good candidate for special judicial solicitude because their violation undercuts the "self-correcting" character of the democratic process, which is one of its greatest virtues. Popular control is assured precisely because through elections the people can change the governors if they do not like the policies handed down. If the political process is corrupted in some way, real popular control may be lost.

Voting rights and freedom of speech are especially critical for this process. If popular elections do not accurately reflect majority desires, then the democratic process is short-circuited. So, for example, when malapportionment occurs, the legislative majority may actually represent only a popular minority. This is an overwhelming obstacle to the self-correction of the process. One cannot tell a frustrated majority to "vote the rascals out," since the distortion of voting power (reducing a societal majority to a legislative minority) is precisely the problem. Likewise, if freedom of speech is denied, and government opponents cannot alert the people to political evils, then the process will not lead to correction of the error.

When the ordinary political process is corrupted in some way, therefore, correction must come from outside. Judges, insulated from the corrupted process by their tenure during good behavior, are in a position to intervene and set the process straight.

The third prong of the *Carolene Products* footnote—protection of "discrete and insular minorities"—is justified on similar grounds, although one must look a bit closer to see why the political process provides inadequate protection. It is not simply a case of minorities' not being able to protect their rights because they are the "losers" in the process. After all, there are always losers when Congress votes on legislation, and often the arguments turn precisely on whether certain rights are being advanced or denied, yet we can hardly invite the judiciary to override the results of the legislative process at will. Exceptional protection is needed only for those minorities for whom the ordinary protections within the normal political process do not work.

What are the facets of the normal political process that provide protection to minorities? Legislation is passed not by a homogeneous majority but by a majority coalition made up of the varied interests (all of which are "minorities") that are part of an extended republic. Coalitions are not permanent; they form and re-form around various issues. Those interests and representatives whose self-interest is not immediately implicated by a given piece of legislation often use their votes on such issues to negotiate support for other issues that do involve their interests. Moreover, the participants in this process know that these groups with whom they disagree on one issue may be necessary to provide the crucial margin for a winning coalition in the future. The coalition-forming process, therefore, contains important moderating features that help prevent minorities from being overridden or completely ignored.

These protections can be undercut, however. First, if minorities are systematically denied a place in the political process (see strand two of *Carolene Products* above), where the negotiation and bargaining and vote-trading take place, they cannot "ante up" to play the political game; they are outside the process and its protections. Second, if a group is easily identifiable, can be isolated from the rest of society, and is subject to long-standing popular hostility or prejudice (i.e., if it is "discrete and insular"), it may lack political representation or the few representatives it does have may not have even the limited ability to protect against deprivations of fundamental rights. For example, no amount of "horse-trading" would induce a representative to vote for equal rights for a political minority that is so unpopular that such a vote would spell political suicide.

Moreover, threats of oppression do not come only from government, although the *Carolene Products* rationale seems to focus on that threat. Sometimes unfair treatment comes from private individuals, and government adds to the problem because it will *not* act. In such situations, the extended republic principle may actually facilitate oppression. If locally oppressed minorities appeal to the larger community for protection, they may find that the same "moderated" processes that make extreme unfair treatment less likely at that higher level also have the effect of making decisive action to protect local minorities unlikely as well. Oppressed blacks in the South were not able to obtain relief from the national government partly because southern congressional representatives were able to take advantage of the legislative branch's nature and processes to defeat or minimize national action.

Again, in such a situation, the argument goes, only a force outside the ordinary political process, and therefore beyond immediate political retribution, is likely to be able to protect even the most fundamental rights of such a minority. That force is modern judicial review. Traditional judicial review is likely to be inadequate because of the sheer ingenuity or power of the oppressive majorities in getting around whatever constitutional clear commands exist to protect minorities. Only if judges are given broad leeway to read rights expansively are they likely to be successful in protecting minority rights.

This last *Carolene Products* strand is particularly influential, in great part because American political culture, despite some elements that have led to denials of rights (e.g., streaks of nativism, hyperpatriotism, and racism), also contains a strong rights-consciousness and an inclination (associated perhaps with our individualism and suspicion of government) to support "the little guy" against both public and private oppressive combinations. America has no formal political position for "ombudsmen" (officials in Scandinavian countries who are responsible for dealing with individuals' complaints of unfair treatment). However, modern judicial power assigns judges a task somewhat like an ombudsman's. The president or senator or representative may not be able or willing to listen to a complaint and give an answer, but courts have to hear cases within their jurisdiction and give answers. Americans are naturally inclined to find that opportunity for a forum valuable.

Insofar as the Court actively undertakes this task of protecting specific constitutional rights, the integrity of the political process, and the rights of discrete and insular minorities, it is fulfilling a task that is absolutely essential to modern democracy with its emphasis on liberty. Therefore, the Court can be fairly considered to be quite democratic in the extremely important realm of its purposes and effects.

Popular Checks on Judicial Power

Moreover, judges are ultimately subject to popular control; they are not "a will independent of the society," to use James Madison's phrase from *Federalist* No. 51.[14] The Constitution contains a range of checks that makes it possible to rein in an undemocratic or unwise Court. First, the judges can be impeached, by a majority of the House of Representatives and two-thirds of the Senate, for "high crimes and misdemeanors," which is a flexible enough term to include the imposition of seriously harmful policies on the nation without adequate justification in popular support or the traditions of the people. Second, Congress controls the size of the Supreme Court and, with the cooperation of the president, it can neutralize or counter an obstructive or tyrannical Court by making as many new seats and appointments as necessary to restore sense. Congress manipulated the size of the Court for political reasons during the nineteenth century,[15] and the threat of Court packing, despite its formal "defeat," was successful in the twentieth century under Franklin D. Roosevelt. Third, Congress controls the appellate jurisdiction of the Supreme Court, and the entire jurisdiction of the lower courts, and can negate Court power in areas where it has been used improperly. Fourth, the Court can simply be disobeyed, indefinitely with the support or inaction of the executive branch and at least for a time without it. If there is widespread resistance to a Court decision, compliance can be secured only with difficulty and over time.[16] Fifth, a Court decision can be decisively overridden by a constitutional amendment, as in the cases of the Eleventh, Thirteenth, and Sixteenth amendments.[17] Finally, the Court's makeup and thereby its action can be determined by the normal exercise of the appointment power. Throughout U. S. history when the Court has offended a genuine and lasting national majority, appointments have eventually been made that change its character. So, for example, in the nineteenth century the Marshall Court gave way to the Taney Court, and in the twentieth century the Laissez-Faire Court gave way to the Roosevelt Court, and the Warren Court gave way to the Burger Court. It is simply not true, then, that judges are not held accountable.

Tacit Consent and Judicial Review

The other defense of the democratic character of modern judicial power is that the American people have given their tacit consent to it. Tacit consent is a necessary part of any democratic theory, at least when the principle of constitutionalism is involved. Otherwise, there would have to be a rule such as Thomas Jefferson proposed, that every generation or so the laws (including the Constitution) automatically expire, thus requiring the new generation to make its consent to the laws explicit.[18] And if new generations can give tacit consent to old constitutions, then there seems to be no logical reason for denying that they can give tacit consent to historical modifications of old constitutions. Especially when amendment makes constitutional change difficult and forces it into indirect channels (as discussed in chapter 1), such change is likely to be either accepted or rejected tacitly.

Have Americans accepted the transformation of judicial review that has occurred? Despite outcries over particular decisions, there has been no successful institutional attack on the Court in recent decades. In fact, according to survey research, the public has more faith in the judicial branch than in the political branches.[19] The Court has not only survived attacks, but it eventually secured broad public support for some of the initiatives that raised the greatest controversy, such as *Brown* v. *Board of Education*,[20] which was ratified and enforced by the 1964 Civil Rights Act, and *Baker* v. *Carr*,[21] the reapportionment "political ticket" that the Court emerged from with enhanced power and popular prestige.[22]

Modern judicial review is not a recent phenomenon. It is at least a half century old. If the old laissez-faire activism is included, judicial activism's life span is twice that. Yet during that time, there has never been a successful effort to modify significantly the nature of the Court's power. There has certainly been opposition to particular decisions and efforts to roll some of them back. But the story of judicial power has generally been one of expanded power, often with the active support of Congress in the form of legislative provisions that incorporate Court decisions and other laws that expand court jurisdiction. This accommodation and support by the legislature is simply a manifestation of popular tacit consent to the modern character of judicial review.

One of the most significant political battles in recent years was fought in 1987 over President Ronald Reagan's nomination of Judge Robert Bork to the Supreme Court. Defenders of judicial activism can point to this event as more evidence for their contention that Americans have tacitly consented to modern, policy-making Court power. Judge Bork's defeat was due to a variety of factors, not the least of which were that the Senate was controlled by Democrats and that Reagan was politically weak due to the Iran-*contra* imbroglio and was drawing near the end of his second term. Nonetheless, even commentators sympathetic to Bork and to judicial restraint had to acknowledge that a key part of the case against Bork was his opposition to certain modern, activist cases, such as the *Griswold* decision, in which the Court had struck down a Connecticut law banning distribution of contraceptives. Moreover, Reagan had put Bork forward, and Bork defended himself, on the grounds of his antiactivist stance regarding judicial power. Critics not only said that Bork was "wrong" about these cases, but more important they accused him of being "outside the mainstream" of contemporary constitutional commentary. Indeed, the differences between his judicial philosophy and many Supreme Court precedents, as well as most contemporary constitutional commentary, led to the charge that Bork was a "judicial activist." Bork's defeat could easily be read, therefore, as a major legislative referendum, not just on the policy implications of his views, but also on whether his views were within the scope of current "legitimate" understandings of judicial power. And he was beaten.

Interestingly, in the wake of the struggle, some right-wing supporters of Bork lamented the way in which Bork had been *defended* during the confirmation process. They said that the *results* of his positions on issues where those results would have been popular (e.g., crime) should have been stressed. But that kind of argument suggests that even some of Bork's supporters have a fundamentally result-oriented approach to judicial power and that they think the American people have such an approach as well.

Although popular understanding of subjects as arcane as the nature of judicial review is extremely limited, tacit consent does not require detailed popular knowledge. If democracy were to require such detailed knowledge, no branch could claim to be democratic. Even public policies supported by huge majorities could be dismissed on the grounds that they are based on "inadequate information." Consistent satisfaction with institutional arrangements, as measured by the best evidence available—no serious efforts to change them—is a valid sign of tacit consent, and by this standard the Court's modern power is more than justified.

For these reasons, defenders of judicial activism argue, the Court cannot be dismissed as undemocratic, or as an anomaly in our political scheme. On the contrary, the Court is vital to the proper functioning of our democratic republic and has clearly established its democratic "credentials."

CRITIQUE OF THE COURT'S DEMOCRATIC CREDENTIALS

Opponents of judicial activism find the preceding arguments unpersuasive. In this section, we look at their responses to each set of arguments.

Judicial Activism Is Democratic in Its Purposes?

Apart from the abstract question of whether democracy has an exclusive title to protect liberty[23] (mixed governments make that claim too) or advance equality (authoritarian governments can do that to a great degree), these democratic purposes leave intact what might be called the structurally antidemocratic character of judicial power. Democracy is not simply government *for* the people; it is *of* and *by* the people as well.

Although certainly liberal democracies like our own value liberty and equality, democracy cannot be defined simply or even primarily in terms of these purposes. What is distinctive about democracy is that it rests on the belief that liberty and equality (and other purposes) are achieved by a certain process; namely, a government that is accountable to the people (i.e., to the majority). Whether judicial activism sometimes brings about greater liberty and equality is not what determines whether it is democratic.

In evaluating this claim that the judiciary's purpose of protecting rights "democratizes" judicial review, we must keep in mind an essential distinction. It is one thing to protect liberty and equality by enforcing specific constitutional rights, as they were understood (broadly) by the framers. The democratic "credentials" in this case derive from the democratic character of the document being carried into effect. Judges enforce the will of the law (the popular will), not their own will. This is the traditional understanding of judicial power, exemplified by the reasoning for judicial review in *Marbury* v. *Madison*.[24]

Modern judicial power is quite a different thing, however. It is the power to define the appropriate extent of liberty and equality under provisions considered to be vague and open-ended constitutional generalities.[25] Most of the important, disputed questions of democratic politics can be formulated as questions of the appropriate extent of liberty and equality. Therefore, modern judicial power is potentially a broad policy-making power. It cannot be minimized on the grounds that it is concerned only with simple "rules of the game" or with a small range of questions, since it deals with many central and substantive political issues.

With this in mind, we can ask the following question: If matters of such importance are at issue, why don't the reasons (whatever they are) for having a fundamentally democratic polity in America apply with as much force to questions involving liberty and equality as to other questions?

We can start to answer this question by asking why Americans have chosen a democratic form of government. Although a number of different formulations might be used to answer this question, one plain, commonsense approach is the following. Americans have agreed that there is no stable readily identifiable, person, group, family, or class (e.g., the rich, the poor, the educated, the old) that can be expected consistently to rule better than the whole body of citizens. In other words, if given ultimate political power, no one group can be trusted to secure the rights of Americans most effectively over time. For example, given human nature as it is, political institutions cannot count on the availability of "enlightened statesmen" who will be able to adjust "clashing interests, and render them all subservient to the public good."[26] Thus, all citizens share in the governance of the community, and the majority will is authoritative. Some people will have more power and influence than others, but this will occur because of their own capacity and effort (or even luck), and with popular consent.

The absence of a legitimate claim to exclusive power by any person or group would seem to apply as readily to important questions defining the appropriate extent of liberty and equality as to other issues. Some issues may have obvious answers, but most of those that become controversial are not so simple to deal with.

The difficulty of such questions should be easy to see. For example, although everyone would like to see the true rights of discrete and insular minorities protected, it is often difficult to determine where the rights in a given policy dispute lie, which minority's rights are most at stake, and whether efforts to protect minority rights conflict with legitimate majority rights. Whose liberty and equality, for example, are at stake in the question of abortion? Is it the woman's right to make decisions about childbearing? Does the father have any rights in regard to his progeny? Is the fetus a human being whose rights must be respected?

Whose rights are at stake in questions of criminal procedure? The right of an innocent person not to be convicted falsely? The right of any person, including the guilty, to a certain form of humane and equal treatment? The right of the victim, both the actual victim and those who may become victims of criminals freed on procedural grounds?

Whose rights are at stake in busing? The rights of black Americans to an equal education? The rights of white and black children not to be bused for considerable periods of time far from their neighborhoods? The rights of parents to choose schools for their children?

Whose rights are at stake in school prayer and school aid cases? The nonestablishment and free exercise rights of nonbelievers or religious minorities who are in the public schools or who are taxpayers? The majority's free exercise rights to have education consonant with their most fundamental beliefs, without coercing minorities, or the rights of minorities or majorities to secure state aid in support of education without being discriminated against because of their religious views?

The same question can be raised about equal political rights and the integrity of the political process. Do majorities have any rights with respect to defining appropriate forms of representation? Is the "one-person, one-vote" principle of apportionment the only legitimate form, since otherwise the voting power of particular individuals would be reduced, as compared to others? Or can liberal democracies fairly apportion with a view toward increasing the representation of minority groups, even beyond their numbers, to provide additional cautions against oppressive treatment?

Freedom of speech is an important principle in democracies, but it does have limits. Where should the lines be drawn? Must democracies tolerate speech that has the explicit purpose of destroying the government (as, for example, the Weimar Republic in Germany tolerated both the Nazis and the Communists, who were dedicated to destroying it)? May communities legitimately ban speech or various forms of expression that do not merely advocate changes in moral standards but, by their very existence and natural effects, undercut the maintenance of those standards (e.g., obscenity in the depiction of both sexual acts and violence)?

Such questions are very difficult to resolve. The question is not simply whether we will choose to abide by our commitment to certain rights, but rather whose rights are at stake and how to resolve conflicting rights.

This argument is not a retreat into moral skepticism. The difficulty of the questions does not mean that there are no right answers. But because there are right answers does not mean that judges ought to be the ones to ascertain and promulgate them in cases involving rights, any more than they have such power over those issues that are left to the ordinary political process.

Thus, in the absence of clear constitutional guidance,[27] questions about liberty and equality are as much subject to the arguments for democracy as any other. If the typical hard questions of politics are resolved democratically, then hard questions about liberty and equality ought to be resolved the same way. They cannot simply be put in a special category and labeled as "appropriate for nondemocratic resolution."

Judges Can Be Checked Anyway?

In theory, there are numerous checks on judges, such as impeachment, constitutional amendment, congressional control of the Court's size and appellate jurisdiction, the appointment process, and the power to disobey. But each check has its problems, and there are some general problems as well.[28]

The first check, impeachment, is obviously very difficult because a majority in the House of Representatives and a two-thirds majority in the Senate is required for convictions. Moreover, firm (and, on the whole, proper) custom reserves impeachment for cases of personal turpitude or "bad faith" political abuses. While Congress does have the power to define "high crimes and misdemeanors," and this phrase is not limited to indictable crimes—it includes political abuses as well[29]—employing it in cases of "good faith but very wrong interpretation" of the Constitution would be an invitation to any Congress that disliked the Court's interpretation to impeach enough justices to change its overall character. The fact that this is generally recognized means that impeachment is normally an unusable check.

Another extraordinary means of checking the Court is constitutional amendment. If there is a sizable and determined minority, however, this is a very difficult process, because it requires the approval of two-thirds of each house of Congress and three-fourths of the state legislatures. Moreover, it is not desirable to have constitutional amendment frequently or for many particular issues. As Madison argued in *Federalist* No. 49, frequent change undermines the reverence for the Constitution that time builds up and that is a useful support for any government.[30] And Chief Justice John Marshall, in a famous passage of *McCulloch* v. *Maryland* (1819), pointed out that the Constitution should be brief and establish only the broad outlines of government, since it would become unintelligible and inaccessible to the people were it too long and detailed.[31]

Congress can also control, by ordinary statute, the size and the appellate jurisdiction of the Supreme Court. Therefore, with cooperation from the Senate and the president, Congress could check the Court by adding new justices or by cutting off its appellate jurisdiction in areas where its decisions had been "undesirable." Although such practices would be technically constitutional,[32] they would be generally undesirable and could be viewed from a certain perspective as contrary to the spirit of the Constitution.[33]

As with improper use of impeachment, these instruments are too "blunt," because they would set precedents undermining judicial independence. They could be used just as easily against good Court decisions, even those that struck down clear violations of the Constitution, as against bad ones. More-over, cutting back on the Supreme Court's appellate jurisdiction would leave interpretation to the lower federal and state courts, with the likelihood of conflicting interpretations. Such diversity would not necessarily be bad in cases in which the constitutional provisions are unclear,[34] but even if uniformity is essential, there is no reason that judges, rather than the political branches, should choose which interpretations to adopt. Where provisions are clear, a uniform interpretation *is* necessary and proper, as a matter of justice—the rule of law, all being subject to the same general rules—and as a matter of political prudence, since a cheerful acceptance of the equal authority of incompatible interpretations could undermine faith in the intel-ligibility and goodness of the Constitution.

The most frequently used check on the Court has probably been the ordinary appointment process, as new presidents and Senates replace justices who resign, retire, or die. Apart from the fact that the timing is subject to chance, popular control through the appointment process is very attenuated. First, selection of a president is based on many factors, and likely Supreme Court nominations is only one factor. Therefore, there is little guarantee (except occasionally perhaps on unusually controversial issues) that the president's own criteria for selection will represent popular criteria as well. And even when a president's criteria generally concur with popular prefer-ences, there may be important areas where they diverge. Second, presidential selection of justices is a difficult task in which the president's hopes are frequently frustrated. One scholar, Robert Scigliano, estimated that fully one-fourth of the Supreme Court appointees failed to meet presidential expectations;[35] perhaps because the appointee's earlier actions in the judicial arena or other areas misled the president, or because the new position permits or encourages the appointees to change their views, or because justices are chosen without knowing what important issues will come before the Court, the result is that appointment is only a limited check.

A final check on the Court is the power of the other branches and of the people to disobey it. Even without the support of the executive branch, areas of the country can simply refuse to enforce a Court interpretation until litigation brings the issue to the Court; this can take a long time.[36] With executive support, it is possible even to defy the Court, since its judgments are not self-executing.[37]

America, however, has "a government of laws, not of men," and disobe-dience to the Court, even if the decision is bad, has the dangerous effect of undermining the rule of law. Such action would strike at the very heart of the Court's legitimate power, encouraging defiance by any group unhappy with its decisions. Perhaps only in the most extreme emergencies could such an action be justified.[38]

Apart from these limitations on each of the particular checks on judges, there are more general ones as well. First, the simple fact that courts can sometimes be checked does not necessarily make them democratic. It is necessary to see the drastic difference between these two situations.

- Situation Number 1: Laws are made by a large, relatively democratic branch of government (Congress), which is subject to popular control through elections at regular intervals. This branch, however, has many internal checks (including the participation of another branch [the executive] in the legislative process) to limit the likelihood of unjust or unwise legislation by requiring deliberation over time and bargaining among many groups to produce the majority coalition necessary to pass a given law. Congress is also subject to an external check by a relatively undemocratic branch (the judiciary), which is not accountable to the people through elections (serving virtually for life) and which has few indirect checks upon it.
- Situation Number 2: Laws are made by a small, relatively undemocratic branch (the judiciary), which has few significant internal checks. It is subject to external checks, however, primarily in the form of action by a relatively democratic branch (Congress). The checking power of the latter branch, however, is limited by a wide variety of internal checks that make quick action unlikely and tend to require a considerable degree of compromise.

The two situations are obviously different in profound ways. In the first situation, the original and extensive constitutional (and extra-constitutional) checks on Congress operate to prevent action that does not have broad popular support.[39] In the second situation, these same checks on Congress operate to limit its ability to check the courts, thus protecting from congressional control (or significantly modifying the scope of congressional control over) the action by the courts that need not reflect broad popular support.[40] In the latter case, the checks mostly check the checker. The shift from the first situation to the second is fundamental. In the first scenario, the status quo generally prevails in major matters unless there is broad public support for change. In the second scenario, major change (within certain limits, of course, because the courts are not free to do anything they like) can be imposed on the country without broad majoritarian support. The latter case is inconsistent with the basic principles of democracy or republicanism.

Second, the long-range character of the most "legitimate" checks on the Court—appointment and constitutional amendment—undermines their efficacy or the likelihood that they will be invoked. As time passes, the precedential weight of undisturbed decisions grows, thus increasing the likelihood that new judges will uphold decisions out of respect for precedent, even when their abstract opinion on the merits of the earlier decision might be critical.[41] This exacerbates the ambiguities of the appointment process. Judges cannot be asked to commit themselves to particular decisions as a condition for their appointment.[42] It is difficult even to obtain nominees' understandings of different constitutional provisions, although custom is probably more restrictive than it should be.[43] Even if a president succeeds in appointing a justice who seems to be opposed to a decision that the president would also like to see overturned, time and the increased precedential weight may lead the appointee to maintain the earlier decision or merely prune it.

More important, though, time gives Court decisions a chance to shape the future political climate in which their fates will be decided. For example, a Court decision can permit the establishment and growth of businesses or interest groups whose self-interest will lead them to fight actively to defend the original decision. Business interests in the late nineteenth and early twentieth centuries supported laissez-faire–oriented Court decisions, especially through a business-oriented legal profession and appointments by presidents with pro-business orientation.[44] More recently, the very possibility of basing a medical practice on the performance of abortions is grounded on the Court's decision in *Roe* v. *Wade* (1973), and therefore certain economic and ideological interests will actively support efforts to maintain that decision and oppose efforts to modify or overturn it. And the Court's civil rights decisions over the past several decades have built up a "court constituency" among civil rights groups whose existence or power would perhaps not have been possible without those decisions.

The point is not that this is illegitimate per se; obviously, groups benefited by the Court's decisions will tend to support it and them. It is simply that there are practical limitations that make the use of some theoretical checks on the Court difficult. Groups that have been or are directly dependent on Court decisions will support the Court with a high level of intensity. In our political system an intense minority is in a good position to use checks very effectively, as Southern representatives demonstrated for decades in their ability to prevent federal intervention in civil rights issues.[45] This was one argument used to justify judicial activism on behalf of civil rights: "the political process cannot operate effectively and so judges must intervene." But one cannot have it both ways. If one attacks the political system because minorities can frustrate ordinary political action to bring about change, one cannot justify judicial action on the grounds that majorities are free to use the ordinary political process to restrict excessive judicial power. The possibility that intense pro-Court minorities can frustrate these checks on the judiciary must be acknowledged.

Besides creating or supporting special interests dependent on their decisions, the Supreme Court also contributes to the long-term political forces shaping opinion throughout the nation. Although Court decisions are only one factor, they do help legitimize or delegitimize certain practices and attitudes.[46] For example, racial attitudes have been substantially modified in the last generation. The Court's outlawing of segregation and its consistent support of most civil rights initiatives have been a major factor encouraging this shift.[47] The shift in attitudes, of course, helps support the political forces that the Court helped set in motion and makes it less likely that those decisions will be overturned.

The Court's contribution to social change is a greater or lesser factor in different areas, but its influence is undeniable. The Court does not necessarily initiate broad social change. Typically, a movement or movements often identified with elite social opinion exist to modify previous laws or mores; these movements slowly gain ground but lack the political muscle to achieve drastic change. The Court, sharing the progressive opinion, intervenes to make the "emerging" opinion the basis of public policy. Once established in the law, the process of social change is accelerated, public opinion shifts more quickly, and the original Court decision is thus "vindicated." For example, the widespread change in sexual mores in the last generation was certainly encouraged by Court decisions of the 1960s,[48] and even the Court's change of face on obscenity in 1973 was nowhere near a reestablishment of the *status quo ante*, since *Miller* v. *California* and *Paris Adult* v. *Slaton* protect a considerable amount of material that would not have been protected in 1958.[49] The legal protection afforded obscene materials has helped change the tone of our society in many ways. As so many moral philosophers have held, mores, the prevailing customs, and the "tone" of a society are essential elements in the formation and maintenance of the moral standards of its citizens, so that a change in them contributes to a long-term change in moral standards, a change that undermines the political forces that oppose the Court's original decisions.[50]

Much the same can be said about abortion, the anti-activist would say. Once a rare and scandalous occurrence, it began to become more public in a number of states in the 1960s. It is now commonplace, in great part as a result of the Court's decision in *Roe* v. *Wade* (1973), which gave constitutional protection to a broad right to obtain abortions. To the extent that many people's moral standards are affected by what they take for granted as ordinary, socially approved parts of life,[51] the legitimization of a controversial practice can contribute to its becoming morally acceptable over time, and thus undermine the forces that oppose it.[52]

In fact, this is one of the arguments sometimes put forward for judicial activism: It is capable of effecting necessary change that has been forestalled by a political process with too many built-in checks. Those who argue for judicial activism on the ground that it can alter the balance of social forces and bring about change not only in short-term policy but also in long-range attitudes cannot argue that this is democratic and legitimate because the decision will be overturned if it is contrary to those attitudes. The question in such a case is who should have the major say in shaping the long-range attitudes of the citizenry.

Court decisions are only part of the explanation for such changes in mores, and they reflect deeper factors. The courts are merely the instruments for making authoritative the libertarian sentiments of the modern intellectual elite in areas of personal morality. Still, the legitimization by the judiciary of formerly prohibited practices is at least a contributing factor for effecting elite opinion in this area much more quickly than possible in the ordinary political process, where the nonelite who cling to traditional moral values have more power. (This point is important especially because of the relative volatility of elite opinion, which changes much more quickly than general public opinion. If initial attempts to bring public policy into line with new elite opinions fail, then perhaps older popular opinions will outlast changing elite opinion.)[53]

Court decisions that legitimize certain practices can also mobilize opponents to these practices in the short run. This occurs not only because the opponents are stimulated to act, but also because the controversy generated by the conflict will make the practice an issue for some people who otherwise would not have considered it.[54] The mobilization of the decision's supporters, however, and the long-run effect of legitimization of practices on social opinion, seem likely to outweigh this unintended consequence.

Again, it is not necessarily bad that Court decisions have these long-term effects. The Court's "educative" role can be used well or poorly. However, opponents of a Court decision who wish to overturn that decision by long-term political action, besides facing ordinary difficulties, such as sustaining political action over a long time,[55] find their own political forces undermined by the decision's effects over time. Thus, the efficacy of checks that take a long time, such as appointment and constitutional amendment, is limited.[56]

The conclusion drawn from this discussion is that the checks on the judiciary are much more limited than they first appear. This should not be surprising, of course, because the framers meant the judiciary to be independent, to be relatively free of control by the political branches and majorities. If the Court could be checked readily, then it would not be able to perform its own checking function (e.g., striking down legislative or executive action contrary to the Constitution). The framers' defense of the democratic character of judicial review was that it would not need to be checked; its democratic credentials lay in the definition of judicial review as the enforcement of the people's will embodied in the Constitution. That defense is not seriously open to modern judicial review, which is essentially legislative in character.

There Has Been Tacit Consent to Modern Judicial Power?

The doctrine of tacit consent is an inevitable part of any stable, long-lived democratic regime. Given the long history of activist Courts in the United States, the absence of institutional reform to prohibit such activism, and the ultimate acceptance of some of its major initiatives by the political branches, can it be said that the American people have tacitly consented to modern judicial review, thus providing it with proper democratic credentials?

Any form of consent, including tacit consent, presumes knowledge of what is being consented to. It is not possible to consent to something that one doesn't understand, and any consent based on a false general understanding is questionable. While the *full* implications of consent can never be known— human beings never know the full implications of anything—at least the *basic principle* of the institution or practice at issue must be clear.

Of course, if pushed too far, this principle raises problems for explicit consent as well. The depth of popular understanding of political issues, for example, even in a debate on the ratification of an explicit amendment to the Constitution, is always subject to some question. But at least a debate on an explicit amendment provides much more "notice" to the people that some aspect of their fundamental political principles is at stake, and thereby provides a more adequate measure of consent.

Opponents of judicial activism argue that Americans have not given tacit consent to the basic principle of *modern* judicial review; that is, to the power of the courts to strike down laws or acts that seem to violate significant rights or to command acts that seem necessary to guarantee such rights, even when there is no clear constitutional prohibition or command. Most Americans still understand judicial review as the power of the courts to strike down laws that violate the Constitution. Moreover, they still think of the Constitution as an intelligible document that grants certain powers and places certain limitations on those powers by means of specific prohibitions. Although most Americans are aware that there is "fuzziness" or uncertainty about some provisions, they do not consider the Constitution as providing a "blank check" to the judiciary to guarantee liberty and equality.

What most Americans think is, of course, impressionistic. Polls can tell us something, but they are notoriously open to variation according to the wording of the question. One suspects that there would be drastically different sets of responses to the questions "Should judges protect our fundamental rights?" and "Should judges have the power to create and enforce new rights, apart from those specified in the Constitution?" although the practical effect of each power would be much the same, given modern interpretations of certain constitutional provisions as vague general guarantees of liberty and equality.

A *Los Angeles Times* survey, December 16–18, 1979, reported that 81 percent of the sample felt that "judges do a good job," 57 percent felt that "judges usually base their decision on their interpretation of the law" rather than allowing their personal beliefs and political opinions to play too great a part in their rulings, and 54 percent felt that "judges have not assumed too much power."[57]

Any doubt that the public's ideas on judges are based on little or no actual knowledge of what they do should be removed by the results of a CBS News/*New York Times* poll, March 11–15, 1982, that asked a question on the Supreme Court and abortion. Remember that *Roe* v. *Wade* is one of the half-dozen most controversial and widely discussed decisions in the Court's history. The survey asked, "Does the Supreme Court permit or does it forbid a woman to have an abortion during the first three months of pregnancy, or haven't you been following this closely enough to say?"[58] Incredibly, 10 percent thought that the ruling *forbids* a woman to have an abortion during the first trimester, and 49 percent had not been following the case closely enough to say.

If, for the most part, the public is unaware of the content of *Roe* v. *Wade*, is there any reason to assume that there is widespread public knowledge of how the modern Court goes about its decision making and how much power it implicitly claims? The latter is an infinitely more complex matter and perhaps beyond the capacity of the average citizen to grasp accurately as long as it is shrouded in the typical descriptions of judicial power. In this regard, the Court's own language is important to note.

Since the turn of the century, the legal profession has commonly observed that judges *make* law; they are essentially legislators. This Holmesian wisdom was so dominant by the 1920s that Benjamin Cardozo, in his famous Yale lectures (later published as *The Nature of the Judicial Process*), could say that he was not concerned about asking whether judges ought to be allowed to decide cases according to "some consideration of the social welfare, by my own or common standards of justice and morals" because "I take judge-made law as one of the existing realities of life."[59] To deny the legislative character of judicial review in discussions among scholars and lawyers today is to invite sharp criticism, or even worse, patronizing condescension for one's naiveté.[60]

Yet for all this, how does the Court describe its role? Only once in a long while will a justice drop from the bench the remark that judges do in fact make law (e.g., Justice Byron White's dissent in *Miranda* v. *Arizona*).[61] Often, especially in big cases like the *United States* v. *Nixon* where popular support may be especially important to secure obedience to the decisions, the Court engages in what noted legal commentator Alexander Bickel called "atavistic regressions to the simplicities of *Marbury* v. *Madison*."[62] That is, the Court maintains that it is simply interpreting the Constitution; that is, enforcing the will of the people embodied therein. This defense could be characterized, some would say, as intellectually dishonest. Modern "interpretation" of the Constitution is not fundamentally interpretive; it consists, not in ascertaining an intelligible meaning and giving it effect in a particular set of circumstances, but in giving specific content to vague generalities that provide little guidance to the judges in their "balancing" of broad competing interests.[63] This expansive judicial power can be defended intelligently, of course, but it cannot accurately be defended as "interpretation," as the Court's *public* defenders in Congress, for instance, or in newspaper editorials that characterize anti–*Roe* v. *Wade* activity as an "attack on the Constitution" often do.

When the Court explicitly and consistently characterizes its acts of judicial review as "legislative" acts, as policy-making; when the Court's congressional defenders consistently resist Court-limiting legislation on the grounds that the Court *should* be an independent policy-maker enforcing its own views of the public good; when the Court's defenders in the media consistently argue that the Constitution means whatever the judges want it to mean . . . then perhaps it will be barely possible to talk about "tacit consent." Even then, whatever support the judges get still may not reflect the deliberative consent of the people to the proposition that the Court's role should be a broad policy-making one. The support may come from those who approve of the present policies pursued by the Court.

Nor does the fact that the Court has survived institutional attacks demonstrate the tacit consent of Americans to modern Court power. The rejection of particular methods of reining in the Court (e.g., modification of appellate jurisdiction over particular subject matter, constitutional amendment) may reflect—besides the effectiveness of internal checks that minorities can use well—a preference for a solution that distinguishes more clearly between the Court's appropriate independence and the abuse of its independence; that is, the Court's voluntary withdrawal from its pretensions. Judicial activism may be tolerated because of the difficulty of devising a check that strikes not only at the Court's improper power but at its legitimate power as well.[64]

Nor does the acceptance of some of the Court's policy initiatives constitute a tacit consent to judicial policy-making power. Opponents of judicial activism might think that the Court was right in some of its policies—and want to maintain them as the policies of the political branches—while thinking that the Court had abused its power by enforcing them. For example, assuming for the sake of argument that the Court did not have the constitutional power to prohibit segregation in education (as Raoul Berger argues),[65] one might approve of the content of that policy and fight to maintain it, while arguing that the Court went beyond its power in *Brown* v. *Board of Education* and its progeny. In fact, strictly speaking, one could agree with the *policies* of most of the modern Court's decisions, while arguing that the Court had (and has) no right to impose such policies. The simple fact that public opinion has supported, or comes eventually to support, many Court decisions does not constitute tacit acceptance of modern Court power.

Did the Robert Bork nomination struggle suggest a broad shift in the public understanding of the nature of judicial review? Opponents of judicial activism would argue that it is difficult to draw any clear conclusion from the tangle of factors that led to his defeat. For example, Bork was clearly hurt by an early 1960s *New Republic* article that criticized the Civil Rights Act of 1964. But did Bork's opponents consider Bork's position bad because it was contrary to (1) their self-interest or political ideology, or (2) a modern, expanded conception of the Constitution, allied to an activist conception of judicial power, or (3) the Constitution, read and interpreted according to its true, inherent meaning ("strictly")? Probably there were examples of each among Bork's opponents (and also among his defenders, not the least of whom was Bork himself, who had repudiated that earlier position, presumably on something close to the third reason). Even if the confirmation struggle was an essentially political battle, fought with a view to the expected effect of a Justice Bork on public policy, that would not prove that the American people have tacitly consented to an activist conception of judicial power.

Liking certain policy results of past activist Court decisions and striving to maintain them in the nomination process is not the same as saying that in general it is *legitimate* for justices to be activist.

Tacit consent is a necessary part of democratic theory, as Madison argued. Its primary use, however, may be to provide a basis for the continuing legitimacy of institutions to which the people have already at some time explicitly consented. To use it to justify major changes may be very dangerous, for the changes that are thus legitimized may not result from sufficient deliberation about potential long-term consequences.[66]

One wonders what defenders of such tacit consent to expanded judicial power would say in the case of, say, tacit consent to a narrowed Bill of Rights. Defenders of judicial activism are often fond of pointing to social science evidence that most Americans have more restricted notions of freedom of speech than the Court.[67] If the Court were to gradually narrow the First Amendment's protections over time, in line with these popular views, would the justices argue that such a change was legitimate because of popular tacit consent? Or would they argue that the absence of genuine public deliberation was a fatal flaw in this attempt to undo the wise provisions of our forefathers?

This completes the first round of argument on the question of whether judicial activism is compatible with the principles of democratic government. In chapter 3, we will continue the debate by examining some of the responses to the arguments of this first round. As we do, I think that there will be a tendency to shift the argument from the grounds of democracy to the broader grounds of good government.

CHAPTER THREE

Judicial Review
and
Good Government

DEFENDING JUDICIAL ACTIVISM

D efenders of judicial activism, confronted with the critique of their position described in chapter 2, could respond on several levels. They might address the limited character of judicial power, the question of the judges' democratic credentials *relative to* those of other institutions and officials whose acts they are reviewing, the good results of using the limited power of the judiciary to resolve difficult questions of liberty and equality and the principled reasons behind this success, and finally the real efficacy of checks on judges.

Keeping the Question in Perspective

We must remember that judges do not have, and do not claim, an unlimited power to define the appropriate extent of liberty and equality. First, there is the case and controversy requirement. Judges do not have a roving commission to seek out and overturn bad laws. The power of judicial review is exercised in the context of a specific case or controversy brought to the courts for resolution. The fact that the courts have to wait for a case to be brought before them is a significant limit on the scope of their power.[1]

Second, the formal and informal checks, such as "legal public opinion" (the legal profession's sense of what is legitimate), ensure that judges cannot and will not do anything that does not have the support of at least a sizeable segment of American society. If the judges did not have a significant measure of popular support, their action could be very quickly overturned, and they are sensitive to these limits.[2] Thus, even the Court's most controversial and most criticized opinions—*Dred Scott* v. *Sandford, Lochner* v. *New York, Brown* v. *Board of Education, Miranda* v. *Arizona, Roe* v. *Wade*—represented widely held views in American society.

Moreover, it takes time and debate within the legal profession before the Supreme Court is willing to make a major policy innovation. Decisions are not an impulsive or arbitrary act but the fruit of considerable thought and discussion—in law reviews, in the political branches, and in lower federal and state courts. And the members of the Court are rather prestigious figures in a profession known for its conservatism, its attachment to forms, its respect for precedent, and its solicitude for established rights.[3]

The point of these remarks is simply to make clear what is well known but rarely acknowledged by opponents of judicial activism, that the power exercised by judicial activists is still very limited. "Judicial despotism," or absolute judicial power, does not exist. Whether it is limited enough is still an important and legitimate question, but the debate must focus on *that* question and not on a strawman case of "unfettered judicial power."

The Judiciary:
Democratic As Compared to Whom and What?

In debates on democracy it is easy to operate with oversimplified notions of what democracy is. *Democracy*, after all, is something of a buzzword in our political culture, used of all good things and opposed to all bad things. But no serious observer believes that any of our institutions are purely democratic or that pure democracy is possible or desirable. The real question, therefore is not whether a given institution meets some purely abstract standard of democracy, but what are the relative democratic credentials of our different political institutions.

In the standard social-studies discussion of the three branches of government, the judiciary comes off as by far the least democratic, because of its mode of selection and, above all, its tenure during good behavior. Once we move beyond civics books to serious discussion of the other branches and to close examination of what judicial review often involves, however, the need for a more nuanced view becomes clear.

The legislature is popularly portrayed as composed of representatives of the people, but there are serious limits to the accuracy of this view. Some limits concern individual representatives; others address the legislative process as a whole.[4]

How representative are the representatives? Just a few of the problems are as follows: How many people know who their representatives are? (Less than a majority.) What percentage of the citizens in the district actually voted for the winner? (Typically, far fewer than a majority even vote.) How much do citizens attend to campaigns and know the issues involved? (The incumbent reelection rate of close to 90 percent for the House of Representatives suggests that name recognition is the key factor in getting elected, with no guarantee that those with the greatest name recognition genuinely represent the views of their constituents on most matters.) How much does the average citizen know about, or even care about, what representatives are doing in Congress? (With the exception of a very small number of salient issues, most constituents know little and care little about what their representatives are doing.) Can we say with any confidence that judges who strike down laws passed by representatives are striking down laws that "the people" favor? (Hardly.)

What about the legislative process? If the representatives could be assumed to be accurate reflections of their constituents' sentiments or opinions, would the legislative process represent the will of the majority? Even a short list of undemocratic features of the legislative process would render that claim very dubious. For example, views favored by the chamber leadership are likely to receive special attention, regardless of whether they truly represent majority views. Committee and subcommittee chairpersons have greater influence over policy than other members, regardless of whether they represent more people. In the House, the small group of representatives on the Rules Committee controls whether and how a bill gets to the House floor after it comes out of committee. In the Senate, which jealously guards its prerogative of "unlimited debate," a filibuster by a minority of senators (who may represent an even smaller minority of the country, given the Senate's equal representation of small and large states) can kill legislation that has majority support.

We are not comparing the judges, then, to the pure "voice of the people," which is how the legislature is sometimes portrayed. There is simply no reasonable guarantee that any given piece of legislation truly represents the will of the majority of Americans. This may not be bad, one might say. The point is, whether you consider it good or bad, the "gap" between the democratic credentials of the judiciary and the legislature is not as great as it might seem.

Much the same can be said of the executive. Although the president is the only official (the vice president hardly counts) elected by the whole people, it would be ridiculous to assume that all that the president does is truly reflective of majority will. People are given a choice between two candidates in the general election for the presidency, and we can safely assume that only a very small number of people will find either one of the candidates satisfactory on all the issues, even if we indulge the fond hope that most voting is genuinely based on the issues. For the vast majority of voters, it is a question of who is better, in their opinion, on most issues or on the most important issues. One could easily enough imagine an election in which many people had to choose between a candidate they usually disagreed with and one they disagreed with even more. Thus, the president may be *more* representative than the candidate he defeated, but there is no reason to assume that many of the policies he pursues will genuinely reflect majority will.

Finally, legislation requires the concurrence of both houses of Congress and the president. The effect of bicameralism and separation of powers is to provide checks that make it less likely that laws will reflect the less representative views of either branch, but this is only "less" likely. These checks can also have the reverse effect of preventing the passage of legislation genuinely favored by a majority.

All in all, then, we must keep in mind that we are comparing the judicial branch to an ordinary political process that has its own kinds of nondemocratic features—not to an ancient Greek city-state's democratic assembly of the whole citizenry. And this comparison significantly reduces the differences between the judiciary and the other branches.

The alleged deficiencies of the judges' democratic credentials pale even further when we actually look at whose actions the judges are striking down in many of the cases they decide. While sometimes a piece of legislation or an act of the president is at stake, often that is not the case.

First, most judicial review involves state acts. Even if it is a state legislative act or the act of the governor, such acts may very well represent a distinctly minority position in the country as a whole. When the Court first held that states must provide counsel to indigent defendants, for example, in *Gideon* v. *Wainwright*,[5] it was hardly imposing a minority view. In fact, the view eventually adopted by the Court was put forward in a brief supported by twenty-two states; Florida's opposing view was joined by only two other states.

Second, many cases involve either federal or state action of other judges or administrative officials or government employees who can make little claim to represent the popular will. When the Warren Court expanded the rights of criminal defendants during the 1960s, was it overriding the will of the people expressed through the ordinary political process? In some cases, the rules that were overturned had been the result of past common law adjudication (i.e., previous judge-made law).[6] Modern Court rulings narrowing the category of the legally obscene often involved overturning judgments about particular books or movies made by local juries in cases brought by local prosecutors under vague statutes.[7] Free speech cases have often involved overriding only the police officials' sense of what constitutes a "breach of the peace" or whether a license to use a park should be granted to a particular, often unpopular, group.[8] Under these kinds of circumstances, one would be hard-put to see in the judicial action a blow against the "will of the people."

Third, some cases involve action that might once have had majority support, but is now totally outdated. The first modern "privacy" case, in 1965, involved a Connecticut law forbidding the dispensing of contraceptives; this law could not possibly have had the support of more than a small minority of the state, and was in fact virtually unenforced.[9] The law was simply a relic of earlier days, but it was difficult to repeal because one interest group—the Catholic Church—was opposed to it, and legislators are afraid to offend such interests. The Court's decision could clearly be considered an effectuation of the real majority will of that state, not to mention the nation. What was being struck down was not the will of the people, but the will of a temporary majority that was long-since dead.

When one considers these factors, the accusation that judicial review is undemocratic is certainly attenuated to a great extent. And the smaller the gap between the allegedly democratic character of laws being struck down and the allegedly undemocratic character of the judges, the more likely it is that we will find the small gap justified by other kinds of arguments. If it could be shown that somewhat undemocratic features of government bring valuable benefits, most of us would be willing to tolerate those features.

"The Proof is in the Pudding," or The Good Results of Judicial Activism

The defender of judicial activism may also rely to a considerable extent on the argument that our experience with it since 1937 has shown that the power has been used quite well. An institution cannot be evaluated simply on the basis of abstract arguments. Whether it produces good results in practice must be an essential part of our judgment, and judicial activism has produced good results.[10]

A typical summary of these results might include the following. First, the Court decision in *Brown* v. *Board of Education of Topeka* was the catalyst that made possible the revolution in race relations that eliminated the scandal of white supremacist legislation, especially segregation, in the South. Southern power in Congress had prevented national legislation from completing the vindication of black rights begun in the Civil War and the postwar amendments, and so the judiciary had to step in to set the process in motion. In so doing, the Court helped the nation realize its own best principles, and it served democratic purposes—and justice—well.[11]

Second, the modern Court has protected freedom of speech and religion, especially for unpopular minorities and in times of public passions. Advocates of judicial activism might have wished for an even more assertive Court during the McCarthy era, for the Court did bow before prevailing winds in some cases.[12] Still, the Court did intervene in numerous cases to strike down congressional acts or to modify them by narrow statutory construction and was able to protect some people who otherwise might have been treated more harshly.[13] The attacks on the Court in the mid-1950s were a measure of the feeling in Congress that the Court had been an obstruction.[14] Perhaps the broad toleration of vigorous dissent during the 1960s was partly a reflection of the expectation that dissenters' rights would be protected by the Court, as they were in the relatively few cases that came up.[15]

Religious minorities such as the Jehovah's Witnesses and Sabbatarians have been protected by the Court. Unable to wield any significant power in legislatures, they have been able to escape discriminatory legislation or enforcement of vague laws only by the Court's intervention.[16]

Third, the Court was the catalyst for removing the antidemocratic scandal of malapportioned voting districts. For a minority to be able to control the legislature violates fundamental democratic principles of majority rule.[17] Yet the nature of the abuse makes it practically impossible for those who suffer from it to use the perverted political process to vindicate their rights. Justice Felix Frankfurter's dissenting phrase is a pretty one—"In a democratic society like ours, relief must come through an aroused popular conscience that sears the conscience of the people's representatives"[18]—but the whole view of human nature on which the Constitution rests suggests that those who have power unjustly will rarely give it up in a spasm of guilt. They are more likely to invent rationalizations for their position than to give it up voluntarily. It took an agent outside the distorted political process to restore its integrity by demanding that the political process reflect majority rule.[19]

Fourth, the Court has protected the rights of another minority: criminal defendants. In so doing, it has protected the rights not only of criminals (and even criminals have rights that must be respected), but also of innocent Americans who might have been unjustly convicted or whose privacy and personal security might have been infringed. How is it possible to deny that the complexities of our law demand that defendants have counsel to ensure a fair hearing?[20] Only a fool (or a lawyer—and a foolish one) would forgo counsel in a criminal case, although states had no problem cheerfully forgoing counsel "for" others (indigents) in state criminal proceedings.[21] A state legislator may have had a greater interest (i.e., reelection) in saving money and being "against crime" than in doing justice in a way that would largely benefit criminals and poor people. Judges who had to preside over appeals of verdicts rendered questionable by the absence of a fair hearing (an adversary process with only one effective adversary) were in a better position to require that justice be done, and so again they stepped into the vacuum left by legislative inaction. They did likewise in the case of unreasonable searches and seizures—providing for more effective enforcement of privacy rights through the exclusionary rule in the absence of serious state alternatives to enforce this right[22]—and improper police interrogation—providing the *Miranda* rule to eliminate "the third degree" and other questionable practices, again in the absence of serious state attempts to enforce the right against self-incrimination.[23]

Finally, the Court forced states to establish some rational framework for the administration of the ultimate penalty—capital punishment—and to limit its application to the most serious crimes. If the death penalty is to be used in a society that claims to value individual rights and the dignity of the person, it is imperative that it not be employed arbitrarily or capriciously. The Court requirements that state guidelines specify conditions that make application of the death penalty reasonable and that they consider mitigating factors are a real improvement over the random pattern of executions prior to *Furman* v. *Georgia*. Moreover, limitation of the penalty to only the most serious crimes—not, for example, simple rape or driving the getaway car in a bank robbery where murder is committed—is appropriate as well.[24]

Fifth, and last, the Court has resisted or overturned the efforts of government to intervene in intensely personal and private decisions that have a major impact on a person's life, without a clear and definite effect on others. Such decisions are said to be the key to "the pursuit of happiness" in a person's life, and our political principles call for the protection of personal autonomy in such decisions, unless they involve clear, direct, tangible harm to others. Thus, the Court has struck down illiberal laws regarding contraception and abortion, which are said to have imposed immense harm on some individuals in the name of other people's moral views.[25]

This catalogue of good results is one of the strongest arguments in favor of modern (post-1937) judicial activism, its proponents argue. Ultimately, any defense of a political institution must be based in some sense on its having good results, and judicial activism has justified itself under that criterion.

Special Judicial Abilities

At the same time, these good results are not accidental; that is, they are not simply due to the fact that some good justices happened to be on the Court at a given time. Supporters of judicial activism argue that these good results reflect a special ability that judges have to decide such questions well. This ability is "special" particularly in the sense that judges, although obviously fallible, are superior to the alternative decision makers, such as the political branches, especially legislatures.[26]

As a group, judges are particularly well educated, especially in the law. While legislators also have above-average education, they are more directly accountable to citizens who often have much less education and a less sophisticated understanding of political questions. Appointment to the Supreme Court, in particular, is often based on legal eminence. (The requirement of some legal distinction was brought home by the reaction—a mixture of disbelief, hilarity, ridicule—to one senator's defense of a nominee—G. Harrold Carswell, nominated by Richard Nixon in 1970—on the grounds of his mediocrity.) Moreover, a large number of appointees to the Supreme Court have had extensive political experience as well, so their knowledge is not simply from a legal ivory tower. Few Supreme Court justices have not had distinguished careers before their appointments; if there are exceptions to this, they are few compared to those who find their way into legislatures with little or no grounds for claiming eminence of any kind.[27]

The judges' special ability to decide questions of constitutional rights also rests on their freedom from political pressure, above all, in the form of self-interest in being reelected. This insulation from the normal electoral process has always been viewed as an essential element in protecting the judges' impartiality. A legislator is not "impartial"—and is not supposed to be—but rather an advocate, a representative of constituents' views. A judge is not an advocate for a particular electoral group, and this independence permits the judge to decide questions on their legal merits.[28]

This is particularly important when it is a question of minority rights. In a case of a "discrete and insular" minority (i.e., one that is readily identifiable and "isolable"), normal electoral politics provide little immediate self-interest for a legislator to run counter to popular dislikes and to defend unpopular minorities. Yet unpopular minorities have rights that must be respected. Judges are in a much better position to defend such rights, because they are free from the pressure of hostile electoral groups. Ironically, judges may be viewed as "impartial advocates" for those who have no effective advocacy in the political process. They are impartial, in that they are free from political pressure to deny minority rights, and they are advocates, in the sense that their protection of minority rights may be the only effective protection for those rights.

The "detachment" of judges from the political process also provides another advantage: the opportunity for greater reflection, which the nature of their profession permits—indeed, demands—of them.[29] The immediate political process, especially the legislative process, gives politicians little time or incentive for reflection. The variety of duties, the sheer volume of legislation, the negotiation and bargaining with interest groups and with each other, the need to keep fences back in the district well mended, all leave the legislator without the time or detachment to deal with issues reflectively: to think back to the first principles of our political life, to carefully weigh the different social interests involved, to arrive at and articulate a reasoned judgment on how to balance the conflicting interests.

Judges are subject to fewer external pressures; they are free from the pressing need to accommodate contrary interests so extensively as to produce legislation of Rube Goldberg incoherence (explicable only on political, not rational, grounds). They are trained to examine legal arguments carefully and critically and are familiar with the development of the law and its present broad contours. The very nature of the law that appellate judges make demands rationality and coherence to provide guidance to lower courts.

Moreover, judges must normally give an elaborate, reasoned defense of their opinions, which is subject to immediate response by dissenters and to long-range response by a host of legal commentators and legal scholarship. Perhaps precisely because judges lack "force" or immediate power, their authority and prestige rest especially on their ability to provide persuasive reasoning for their actions.

Thus, it is not surprising that judges have been successful in their efforts to provide reasonable protection for liberty and equality. The success of their efforts represents the logical outcome of their special abilities, and this in turn provides a broader justification for judicial activism.

The Reality of the Checks

Contrary to the suggestions of opponents of judicial activism, the checks on the judges are very real. Much of the argument against their efficacy takes the form "we concede that judges *can* be checked this way, but we are reluctant to do so because these methods (impeachment, control of appellate jurisdiction, Court-packing, disobedience, etc.) may be abused." The simple answer is that any power may be abused, but that should not prevent the power from being used if other serious abuses need correction. If the opponents of judicial activism acknowledge that judicial abuses are not serious, they give up the main thrust of their case. If they contend that such abuses are serious, then there is no adequate ground for being reluctant to use the weapons that are available to limit the judiciary. This suggests to the judicial activist that the real reason that checks are "ineffectual" is that opponents of the judiciary do not have broad popular support for their belief that judges have seriously abused their power.

Moreover, checks on the judiciary have been used successfully. Control of appellate jurisdiction and manipulation of the size of the Court, for example, were used in the post–Civil War era.[30] President Roosevelt's Court-packing plan succeeded, not by being passed, but by inducing the judges to change their course in midstream.[31] Likewise, threats of action against the Court seem to have had a significant impact on what the Court has done at certain times, even since 1937. The Vinson and Warren Courts of the 1950s and the Burger Court of the late 1970s had to exercise some care in the use of their powers due to popular feeling and potential congressional action.[32]

The most effective check has been the long-range check of the appointment power. The Marshall Court did give way to the Taney Court, the laissez-faire Court did give way to the Roosevelt Court, the Warren Court did give way to the Burger Court. If there is widespread popular hostility to what the Court is doing, then eventually the Court will be brought under control.[33] It is not the checks on the judiciary that are ineffectual, but the attempts of certain Court opponents to employ them.

Nor are the more general arguments about the checks on the judiciary valid. It is an oversimplification to say that judicial activism makes possible major change without popular consensus, while legislative action requires broad consensus. First of all, although some congressional action requires broad consensus, much of it does not. For example, one piece of congressional legislation struck down in recent years was a provision in a federal law providing construction grants to religiously affiliated colleges. The provision limited to twenty years the restriction of the building to secular activities. Was this obscure provision the product of broad popular consensus? Even where the broad end of a law has popular support, most Americans may not know or care about the particular means. Moreover, whole categories of legislation may go unnoticed by the majority of the country and cannot be said to represent "broad popular consensus."[34]

Second, judicial activism more typically prevents action than imposes it. Judicial review is primarily a nay-saying power that prevents oppressive majority (or minority) action rather than imposes broad action. Judicial review typically either forbids certain government action or says that if the government does act, it must treat people who are similarly situated the same. If in a certain sense, this "imposes" some broad policy on the nation, it is only a policy that is inherent in some general way in the principles on which the country rests (e.g., equal protection).

The other general argument is that Court decisions help shape the future majorities that will decide whether to employ the checks. But if long-run popular opinion conforms to the Court's initial judgment, how is this a democratic criticism of the Court? Wouldn't this be a *vindication* of the Court's action, which demonstrates that over time the wisdom or justice of the Court's decision has become perceptible to a majority that may have, at first, opposed it? This is an example of the Court's leadership in prodding the nation to see the implications of its general principles more clearly and helping the nation to be more "itself."[35]

RENEWED CRITICISM
OF JUDICIAL ACTIVISM

The opponents of judicial activism would still insist that what is being considered in this debate is not a narrow or very limited power to define appropriate limits for liberty and equality, but in essence a broad power to revise the Constitution. Of course, it is limited in some sense, but not in the crucial sense that it cannot frequently lead to antimajoritarian legislation of considerable importance.

Judges are limited to "cases and controversies," just as they have been limited by the "political questions" doctrine. In fact, however, recent judicial history is a demonstration of the manipulability of the case and controversy requirement just as it is a demonstration of the decline of the political questions doctrine.[36]

Two cases provide transparent examples. *Flast* v. *Cohen*[37] involved a taxpayer suit against spending that was said to violate the First Amendment establishment clause, applied to the states by the Fourteenth Amendment. The Court has traditionally rejected taxpayers' suits on the grounds that the *personal* interest of the taxpayer *qua* taxpayer is negligible, providing an insufficient interest to make a "case" in the sense of that requirement. *Flast* allowed an exception to this general rule by creating a complex, and not particularly persuasive, distinction between *Flast* and previous cases. It is hard to come to any conclusion other than that the Court wanted to carve out an exception that would allow it to take certain kinds of cases that it might otherwise not be able to take.[38]

The second example needs only a bare recital to make clear how the case and controversy limits have been contracted. In considering the standing of environmental groups to challenge the refusal of the Interstate Commerce Commission to suspend a temporary railroad surcharge on most freight rates, the Court said in the *United States* v. *SCRAP*

> that a general rate increase would allegedly cause increased use of nonrecyclable commodities, as compared to recyclable goods, thus resulting in the need to use more natural resources to produce such goods, some of which resources might be taken from the Washington area, and resulting in more refuse that might be discarded in national parks in the Washington area.[39]

Since SCRAP members breathed Washington air and used its forests, rivers, streams, mountains, and other natural resources, they claimed to have standing. Incredibly, the Court agreed.

While the Burger Court has reimposed certain case and controversy limits,[40] the point of these cases is that the Court has the power to manipulate them if it desires. Thus, the case and controversy "requirement" can hardly be viewed as a significant limit.

Judges can rarely make significant decisions without the support of at least a large segment of society. (Perhaps it would be better to modify that statement, however, to "without the tolerance" of a large segment of society.) But should this fact reconcile frustrated majorities, or even "possible" majorities, especially in cases where the obstruction of majority will is not subject to change through elections? The laissez-faire Court had the support of a significant segment of American society. Did that reconcile a frustrated Roosevelt and his legal followers? Should it have?

Nor is it possible for the judiciary to embark on major policy changes without some time for support to build in "legal public opinion" for such a change. But sometimes it may not take too much time. *Roe* v. *Wade* was the result of a relatively short, incomplete evolution of constitutional views on "privacy," the first real precedent being only eight years old at the time of this decision.[41] Moreover, there is the question of whether Americans want to be ruled by the legal profession and its "public opinion"? If the answer is yes then Americans were rather unreasonable in objecting to laissez-faire jurisprudence, for that was in great measure a *creation* of the legal profession.[42]

Still, an important decision that has taken some time to gather support in the legal profession and that commands the support of a significant or large segment of American society may be profoundly antimajoritarian: in the sense either that it does not represent majority desires or that it is not subject to approval and repeal by the majority's elected representatives.[43]

The Results

The argument that the results of judicial activism are good and thereby provide the proof of its utility is questionable.[44] While the Court has made decisions with quite good results, it has made some very unfortunate ones as well. First, with regard to each case typically cited as a good result, another case or judicial principle can be cited that many people would criticize. *Brown* v. *Board of Education of Topeka* ended segregation in southern public schools, in conjunction with action by the political branches in the form of the Civil Rights Act of 1964 and threatened cut-off of federal aid to education.[45] Later cases, however, imposed the very unpopular policy of busing on the country as a remedy, with at least doubtful results.[46] Although it is clear that busing has been opposed by a large majority of Americans (including blacks),[47] it is not at all clear that it has helped to improve educational opportunities for blacks or to improve racial attitudes.[48] Nor is it clear whether the Court's upholding of affirmative action is beneficial in its support for minorities or harmful or dangerous in setting a precedent for specifically race-based legal classifications and for racial quotas.[49]

If freedom of speech has been protected, especially for certain minorities, it is not clear that judicial protection of "speech" such as pornography has been beneficial. Although the Court has backtracked somewhat in this area, its earlier decisions helped unleash a flood of such material in the 1960s and create a whole new public atmosphere or tone regarding sexual matters—a tone clearly inimical to traditional sexual mores and supportive of increased promiscuity (at a time when illegitimate teenage pregnancies have been increasing dramatically).[50] Moreover, much pornography has been coupled with violence, so that at least one wing of feminism has joined in support of some anti-pornography laws.[51]

If freedom of religion has been protected, especially for certain minorities, it is not clear that the overall effects of the Court's decisions in the establishment and free exercise areas have been good. The Court's decisions have been an inconsistent hodgepodge, both within the establishment and free exercise areas and also between the two areas. (Almost everybody, therefore, would be unhappy about some cases.)

In establishment cases, the Court has upheld bus transportation and textbooks for parochial schools and church property tax exemptions, while striking down teacher salary supplements and tuition reimbursement and tax deductions in certain forms. In free exercise cases the Court has created religiously based exemptions from certain employment laws and compulsory education laws, while defending the refusal to provide exemptions for Sabbatarian businesses from Sunday closing laws or for selective conscientious objectors. Some of its free exercise exemption requirements contrast starkly with some of its establishment limitations; for example, the "advancing" of religion by permitting nondiscriminatory state aid to private schools (including religiously affiliated ones) would seem to be as indirect as "advancing" Sabbatarian religions by giving them a benefit not available to others (i.e., collecting unemployment compensation while refusing to accept jobs requiring work on Saturday).[52]

Most important, however, the Court's decisions have thoroughly secularized public education while constricting legislative efforts to effectuate broader opportunity for private, nonsecular education. Thus, its policy has had the practical effect of decreasing educational choices for parents, especially less well-off parents whose religious beliefs make them uncomfortable sending their children to the secularized public schools.[53]

The Court eliminated "crazy-quilt" apportionment, which was simply the result of chance (the maintenance of old apportionment despite drastic population shifts), but then went on to outlaw any scheme that did not conform to its mathematical idea of democracy. Even a popular referendum approving a state constitutional amendment to allow one house of the legislature not based on the "one-person, one-vote" principle, in order to facilitate other kinds of representation by political subdivisions, geographical areas, economic interest, and so on, had to be struck down, the Court said.[54]

Without the Court's intervention, certain criminal defendants' rights would not exist or be enforced. Undoubtedly, some innocent people who might have been convicted have been protected, and the privacy rights of others, especially against unreasonable searches and seizures, have been preserved. Equally undoubtedly, criminals who would otherwise have been convicted and imprisoned have been freed and committed new crimes, and others who might have been deterred from crime by more rigorous enforcement of laws in the courts have done the same.[55]

Finally, there has been less public interference in the right to "privacy" in the form of judicial defense of abortion. The burdens on women carrying to term children they did not want to bear and the threats to maternal health from illegal abortions may have been mitigated. The cost of this: the killing of millions of very small beings, who can only be described as human beings, whether or not the law chooses to regard them as "persons."[56]

For every decision that has brought benefits, in the view of many people, there is a decision that has brought harm, in the view of many others. The "results" of judicial activism, by any fair accounting, are ambiguous.

But there are broader problems with the claim of judicial activism's "good results." The practice of judicial activism is not limited to the post-1937 Court, which has concentrated its efforts on expanding civil liberties and certain forms of social and economic equality. A whole generation of judicial activism prior to 1937 had pursued rather different goals: the defense of economic liberty. This accounts for the fact that most judicial activists prior to 1937 were conservatives, while most advocates of judicial self-restraint, and bitter opponents of judicial activism, were liberals. If judicial activism is to be defended on the basis of its good results, is there any basis for simply ignoring the results of the pre-1937 judicial activism?[57]

As a practical matter, the defenders of judicial activism seem to assume a progressivist stance here: The country has progressed beyond the defective laissez-faire ideology that accounted for pre-1937 economic due process, and there is no likelihood of its returning to that outmoded manner of thinking.[58] Thus, it is sensible to evaluate judicial activism in its contemporary form, since 1937.

History is not kind to such progressivist assumptions, however. Finding patterns of past history has not provided any sure handle for predicting the future. There is simply no sound reason to *assume* that judicial activism will be used for the same purposes in the year 2000 as it was in 1937 or 1954 or 1965. What will the defender of contemporary judicial activism say if in the future the Court not only backs off its present libertarianism and egalitarianism but moves in different directions? Could the New Deal era of broad economic regulation be succeeded by a strong antiregulatory impulse? Could a Court use the due process clause to strike down not only laws prohibiting abortion but also laws permitting it? Could equal protection be used to prohibit affirmative action and race-conscious remedies for past discrimination?

There are at least some signs that future judges could adopt an activist stance quite contrary to the now-prevailing one. Recent years have seen the development of a more conservative, property rights activism in some quarters of legal scholarship. The constitutional clause prohibiting the taking of private property for public purposes without just compensation, for example, was in a dormant state during the Roosevelt, Vinson, and Warren Courts; but in the later Burger Court and now Rehnquist Court it seems to be growing in importance. The legal scholarship behind this development suggests that the implications of an exhumed takings clause could be extraordinary, amounting to a repeal of the welfare state, among other things.[59] (Although even its proponents do not argue that these theoretical implications of the clause should be fully acted on in practice, how far judges might go in using it is uncertain. Even "modest" applications of the clause would be likely to leave in their wake many angry and bitter egalitarians, who typically have found activist judicial review quite congenial.)

How much of the support for judicial activism on the part of those who like its present results is due to the facile assumption that their views will continue to prevail? In this regard, it might be worthwhile to look at a classic book on due process by Rodney Mott, published in 1926. Besides summarizing the previous generation's use of due process to protect economic liberty and property rights, Mott looked forward confidently to a creative jurisprudence that would find new ways of expanding this protection.[60] Yet twelve years later that jurisprudence was dead and the Court was on its way to using substantive due process for quite different goals: applying an increasingly libertarian First Amendment interpretation to the states via the Fourteenth Amendment due process clause.

A more radical defense of judicial activism's results from 1890 to the present entails assumptions that are historicist rather than progressivist. Each generation's standards are proper for that generation. Protecting economic rights was a useful thing in the earlier era of burgeoning capitalism, but it inevitably and properly gave way to a different judicial philosophy when new historical circumstances arose.[61]

Of course, then the questions arise, When did those new historical circumstances appear? and When did the Court respond to them? The era of rising capitalism by and large preceded judicial activism, which was established at a time when large corporations had become powerful and, in retrospect, did not particularly need extraordinary judicial assistance. From the very beginning of laissez-faire activism, its opponents argued that it was based on older economic philosophies increasingly questioned by modern Americans. But it took thirty-two years to vindicate Justices Harlan's and Holmes's dissents in *Lochner* v. *New York* and return such questions to the ordinary political process.

Even if the historicist assumptions were correct in denying the permanent relevance of all but the broadest or most general principles (liberty, equality, self-government), what grounds are there to believe that the Court will enforce the right principles at the right time? If some courts have correctly perceived the wave of the future and ridden the crest of that wave (e.g., *Brown* v. *Board of Education of Topeka*), others have not had notable success in similar attempts (e.g., *Lochner* v. *New York*). Again, even on historicist assumptions, will *Roe* v. *Wade* be the *Brown* or the *Dred Scott* of the future? Are judges particularly adept at prophecy, judging from their historical track record?[62]

Ultimately, the defense of judicial activism on the basis of its good results flounders on the strikingly different results that judicial activism has had over time. Activism's defense, then, typically comes down to the confidence of those who like the present results and who hope to continue obtaining their political goals more effectively through the judiciary than they would be able to through the ordinary political process.

Judges' Special Abilities or Expertise

We must continue to keep in mind here that we are not dealing here with simple traditional judicial review, which was based on interpretation of an intelligible document. We are asking about the pros and cons of judicial activism, which is not judicial enforcement of clear constitutional commands but rather judicial specification of vague general principles, and which is in practice equivalent to a revisory power over the Constitution: modifying it, adding to it, not being bound by the framers' intentions or by any determinate "meaning" of the its provisions.

Judges are usually well educated, especially in the law. But the democratic principle denies that any particular quality, including education, gives grounds for some to rule others without their consent. Were education given a very special status in our polity, as a basis for political authority, then presumably voting would be conditioned not merely on a literacy test but on a stricter test of education. The citation of higher levels of education as a basis for higher levels of political authority is a typical defense of aristocracies, not democracies.

Nor is the democratic distrust of education as a basis for political authority altogether unfounded. Like every other identifiable class of human beings, the educated can be bad rulers, from either self-interest or error. The educated have their own self-interest: to maximize their power and prestige in politics and society. And this is connected with material benefits as well.

In many ways, the recent neoconservative analysis of the "new class" suggests that different kinds of benefits accrue to the educated, especially to those who are adept at manipulating symbols, and judges appear to fall easily within this class.[63]

Nor are the educated necessarily more preserved from error than their less educated fellow citizens. For example, a higher level of formal education might mean a greater indoctrination in the errors of prevailing academic ideologies. After all, who "led the charge" for judicial defense of property rights during the last part of the nineteenth century? Was it not the highly educated members of the bar, who were more fully initiated into the wisdom of laissez-faire economic and political philosophy?[64]

Besides their education, judges are also said to possess a certain impartiality, since they are free of political pressure and reelection self-interest, which can distort the views and actions of other political actors, such as legislators and executives. It is true that judges are more independent; they were meant to be, although not for the purposes of modern judicial activism (i.e., not to make them free to legislate on behalf of certain vague ideals). Independence makes possible impartiality, by permitting judges to follow the law rather than be diverted from it by political pressure. But independence does not guarantee impartiality if the judges make the law rather than apply it according to its framers' intentions, or some other more determinate meaning. If judges are thus free, at least within broad limits, are their views necessarily more impartial than those of legislators and executives, or of popular majorities?

Political pressure is not a bad thing intrinsically. It makes democracy possible, especially through elections. If political pressure is to be avoided, then so is democracy. A legislator is therefore not inferior to a judge as a decision maker simply because he or she is more subject to political pressure. In fact, on grounds of democratic theory, this sensitivity to political pressure is the reason the legislator merits decision-making power.[65]

Even assuming for the sake of argument that judges are more "disinterested" than legislators because self-interest in the form of reelection concerns is not a factor in their decisions, it would be questionable whether this justified judicial activism. It would do so only if self-interest were *the* great danger in politics. Unfortunately, while self-interest can be terribly dangerous, human beings are capable of doing just as much damage to themselves and each other on the basis of the noblest motives.[66] "Good intentions" are perfectly compatible with great ambition, perverse ideology, gross incompetence, or dangerously unreasonable expectations that lead to actions that ultimately magnify social ills rather than decrease them.

It is probably true that in the past the circumstances of judging have typically allowed for a certain "leisure" or time for reflection that is difficult or impossible in the hurly-burly legislative process. If that is still true, however, it is only to a greatly attenuated extent. Today, the workload of a modern Supreme Court justice is, by all accounts, enormous. In 1982 seven of the nine justices spoke publicly about the problem—an unprecedented act. The Court has dealt with the problem over time partly by assigning a larger role to law clerks and by using more of them, and in recent years by forming a "cert pool" among six justices to reduce the workload of deciding which cases to hear. Long gone are the days when the Court would listen to arguments in one case lasting a full week and would decide 60 cases a year. The Court has to deal with 5,000 cases a year now, of which under 300 will be decided on the merits, perhaps 150 with full briefing, oral argument (for one hour), and opinions. While the justices may have a somewhat greater degree of leisure than legislatures, the difference should not be exaggerated.[67]

Judges also have to give a rational defense of their decisions and face criticism from their peers in the legal profession, thus injecting an element of rationality into their political process that may be absent, or at least less present, in the legislative process. But the legislative process typically has a rational element too, as can be seen from the voluminous committee reports on legislative matters summarizing the reasons for proposed legislation, and including the committee members' dissenting views.[68] Final legislative action may be less coherent, often reflecting the battle of various interests and the need to obtain a consensus, or at least a majority coalition, through negotiation and compromise. Modern Supreme Court decisions, however, are clearly subject to frequent charges of incoherence, both within a given opinion (as a result of negotiations and compromise on the Court) and with respect to the precedents that the justices claim to be applying or distinguishing. It is unclear, moreover, whether the price of somewhat greater rationality—limiting the discussion and especially the decision making to nine people—is worth the loss of diminished representation and participation in the decision.

Again, the fact that judges face legal public opinion in the form of criticism of their opinions may provide an incentive to write good, rational opinions, but it may also orient them to the prevailing ideology of the legal profession (e.g., laissez-faire economics in the latter part of the nineteenth century). Moreover, the standard of "rationality" would be a more substantial criterion if it were the relation of judicial opinions to some clear, limited principles of the Constitution. But the Constitution today is regarded as malleable enough to justify almost anything that a group of lawyers considers essential for justice (e.g., through due process or equal protection rationales), and therefore such a standard of rationality does not really add much to the judges' claim of special competence.

Judges' Special Disabilities

Not only can one that doubt that judges have special expertise or ability to legislate in regard to broad constitutional principles, but one can argue that judges have distinct disabilities. First, questions involving the appropriate extent of liberty and equality often require certain kinds of factual knowledge in politics, economics, or sociology that a legal education does not necessarily provide. Whether the Constitution permits states to assign children to school on the basis of race is a legal question of constitutional interpretation, which the judges should be able to handle. Whether court-ordered busing improves educational opportunity for minority groups is an empirical question that can be answered only on the basis of sound analysis of evidence, not on the basis of the Constitution. It is doubtful that judges have any special competence (relative to legislators) to answer such questions.[69] Nor does reliance on "social science evidence" in their opinions, or on special masters appointed by courts in complex issues, obviate this problem. There is almost always social science evidence on both sides, and there are almost always experts on both sides to serve as masters. Choosing the "objective evidence" or the "experts" is controversial as well, and ideological views are likely to have a significant impact.

Second, legal thought tends to see things in terms of "rights," which can cause problems in certain kinds of cases or issues. Determination of abstract rights tends to downplay important "practical" considerations such as how much something *costs* in relation to the benefits that can reasonably be expected and whether achievement of the rights may have side effects that worsen the situation. Judges can try to weigh such facts, but cost–benefit analysis is not necessarily done any better in a court than in a legislature, and the *indirect* consequences of action to secure rights may be more easily overlooked in the courts than in the legislature, where there is greater representation of varied interests.[70]

Moreover, "rights" have a kind of "solidity" or moral stature that makes them much more difficult to modify on the basis of unsatisfactory experience than "interests." Although it is not easy to change public policy in a legislature either, adjustment of policies in the light of experience is not uncommon. Once the Court has found or created a new constitutional "right," it is difficult to modify the principle, even in the face of widespread criticism.[71] The Court does change its mind and overrule itself from time to time, but in the period of judicial activism such overrulings have most frequently been in cases where the Court had once said there was *not* a given right and now there *is*. The major exception to that—the Court's retreat from protection of economic rights after 1937—was the rare occasion of a virtual constitutional revolution.

Third, litigation with concrete adversaries may give content to abstract questions, but it may have several limitations as well. The adversarial legal process may not be the best way to accommodate competing interests, because there is usually a winner and a loser. The legislative process tends to produce compromises. Given the complexity and ambiguity of most political questions, this tendency to force compromise, which is necessary to obtain the coalitions to form legislative majorities, has been viewed as a great strength of the American political system.[72]

Although some negotiation occurs on the Court, the normal judicial process encourages litigants to fight it out by giving them a reasonable hope that they will get their way without compromise, which they frequently do. Litigants challenging government action are usually unhappy with the action of the political process; that is why they go to court. And again, the fact that much court action deals with issues in terms of "rights," with the kind of moral imperative usually attached to them, tends to undercut forces encouraging compromise.

The very concreteness of litigants may also be a potential problem in dealing with "public law" issues. Often cases involving modern constitutional rights require the balancing of the particular rights of an individual against a broad but less tangible social interest. The very tangibility of the individual's claim may be an advantage, especially since broad interests, judges can argue, almost always seem to be substantially attainable through somewhat narrower means.[73]

The relative intangibility of the advantages or benefits of federalism, for example, helps explain the modern Court's assault on that principle. When comparing the general benefits of leaving issues to be decided by diverse states with the concrete harm done to specific individuals, in cases before it, the Court has tended to be more sensitive to the concrete harms than to the general, less tangible advantages of federalism.[74]

Finally, another problem with judicial legislation arises from the fact that judges often decide cases with reference to their specific facts. In one way, this may be useful, since it seems to limit the breadth of Court opinions and therefore does not extend the judicial authority over as wide an area as broader opinions might. But this can also lead to case-by-case and increasingly ad hoc adjudication, which can leave the state of the law constantly unclear and create serious problems regarding the rule of law.[75] If one of the reasons for having law is the need for predictable, uniformly applied rules, rather than ad hoc decrees that leave a citizen uncertain and subject to partiality or inconsistency in enforcement, then case-by-case judge-made constitutional law is open to considerable criticism. This is especially true in circumstances where (1) precedent is openly disregarded, as under the Warren Court, (2) precedents are maintained and distinguished though their spirit is at odds with the new rulings, as during the Burger Court years, (3) the Court is often divided in its reasoning, and (4) the principle of law at issue is nebulous to begin with (e.g., the modern understandings of due process and equal protection).

If judges have certain advantages arising from the nature of their activity, they also have certain disadvantages. Even if Americans had decided to secure the "bevy of platonic guardians" eschewed by Learned Hand,[76] the judiciary would not be the appropriate place to go. Judges may indeed have certain virtues that are called forth and developed by the nature of their task, but those virtues do not constitute an adequate ground for subjecting the political process to them in cases where they do not act with a clear constitutional basis.

The Limited Efficacy of Checks on the Judiciary

Although there are checks on the judiciary that can be used in theory, they were not constructed to serve the function now advocated for them. Impeachment, for instance, was intended to deal with substantial breaches of public trust, with "usurpations" of power.[77] Given that the judges were the "least dangerous" branch when they were limited to judging and precluded from legislating, as in the traditional era, the only kind of checks needed were those dealing with substantial derogations from judicial duty. Gradually over time, judicial power in America has assumed a whole new form that is fundamentally legislative in character. The evolution was so slow that there is still no broad public understanding that it has changed. But the end result is that the judiciary is enormously powerful and its day-to-day functions require an effective check, no less than the ordinary power of Congress and the presidency. Checks designed to handle a sudden or massive usurpation of power or breach of public trust are ill-suited for supplying the new check that would be appropriate for this new situation.[78] Thus, impeachment *can* be used, in theory, but it is entirely too blunt an instrument, because it would threaten the proper independence of the judiciary if used as a kind of "normal" check rather than as an extraordinary one.

The same is true of control of appellate jurisdiction. I know of no statement by the framers that suggests that this power was intended to serve as a check on the judiciary, especially by depriving them of jurisdiction over controversial matters where they had made poor constitutional decisions.[79] The power does exist and may be legitimately used to check the Court,[80] but again it is an inapt instrument, because it is entirely too blunt to use regularly. The same can be said of congressional regulation of the size of the Court.

So, there are checks on the Court, but the question is are they really *usable*? The answer is not very; even opponents of the Court's expansion of power are not willing to deal with that problem by steps that may also gut the Court's legitimate power. They prefer to return to the original constitutional arrangements by persuading the Court, which means persuading the legal profession, that a voluntary withdrawal from its expanded power is the proper course. This course would take longer but may be wiser. Moreover, since the Republican Senate faced this problem first during the impeachment trial of Samuel Chase in 1805 and acquitted themselves nobly by acquitting him, this reluctance to use blunt instruments has become a firmly entrenched constitutional custom, as Roosevelt discovered when he tried to pack the Court.[81]

Although judicial activism is often defended on the grounds that Congress can check the Court, judicial activists are often in the forefront of opposition to the use of those congressional powers, not merely because it is wrong to do so in the given case, but because it is "a threat to the Constitution."[82] That is, they deny the legitimacy of those checks, while using their existence as an argument to support judicial activism (i.e., on the grounds that after all, judicial power is limited). This smacks a bit of having your constitutional cake and eating it too.

Appointment

How effective is appointment as a check? It can clearly rein in the Court, as seen in the cases cited by the defenders of judicial activism: the Taney Court following the Marshall Court, the Roosevelt Court following the laissez-faire Court, the Burger Court following the Warren Court. But two significant problems remain. First, the process can take a long time to become effective. Chief Justice John Marshall dominated the Court for twenty-five years, and led it for thirty-five years, after the political branches came under the control of the Republican party. The laissez-faire Court lasted two generations (1890–1937) and was broken only by a popular president in the midst of a national crisis.

Second, the appointment process rarely undoes previous decisions; rather it tends to prevent the extension of those precedents. Most of Marshall's major decisions were unaffected by the Taney Court, which continued to uphold judicial review, including federal review of the highest state court decisions, and to use the contract clause to strike down about as many state laws as the Marshall Court had. The Taney Court did prevent the extension of Marshall's contract clause principles (e.g., in *Charles River Bridge* v. *Warren Bridge*, continuing a process begun during Marshall's tenure in *Ogden* v. *Saunders*), and cut back exclusive federal power in state regulation of commerce (e.g., in *New York* v. *Miln* and eventually in *Cooley* v. *Board of Wardens*).[83]

The Burger Court, despite its supposed conservatism in relation to the Warren Court liberalism, also was a mixed bag. In a few constitutional areas, it explicitly cut back on precedents from the Warren Court, notably in obscenity,[84] or it created new, more conservative doctrines, as regarding federalism in *National League of Cities* v. *Usery*.[85] In many more areas, the Burger Court nibbled away at the edges, especially in criminal defendants' rights cases,[86] or maintained Warren Court precedents with a narrow refusal to apply their logic to new cases (e.g., restricting the "fundamental rights" category of equal protection law).[87] In some other cases, the Court extended Warren Court precedents considerably (e.g., "privacy" and abortion, and some areas of equal protection).[88] Finally, in other areas, it handed down decisions that were extensions *and* decisions that were restrictions of Warren Court developments (e.g., First Amendment cases, in speech and religion and in busing).[89] The net effect of the Burger Court was certainly not to reverse the Warren Court or to move in the opposite direction, for the most part. Of all its decisions, it will most likely be remembered for *Roe* v. *Wade*.[90]

Although appointment can be effective up to a certain point, it is quite limited, judging from the historical examples of its use. The most effective use came under exceptional circumstances, during a national crisis, the Depression, and under a very popular president. Other typically cited examples of appointment turn out, on examination, to have limited the Court's power primarily by reducing the number of new Court initiatives or preventing the extension of older ones. Moreover, even these partial limitations usually took time.

Nor is it *necessarily* a vindication of the Court if future majorities are brought around to the Court's views and embrace them. To the extent that future majorities are formed in great measure by the actions and practices of previous eras, who gets to direct that formation is a serious question. If a racist Court enforced racist policies that helped promote racist attitudes in society, so that future generations ultimately "vindicated" the original decisions, would that be acceptable to judicial activists, apart from their opposition to the content of the opinions? Absent a constitutional basis for decisions that help shape the attitudes of future generations, there is no democratic rationale for the Court to impose policies that shape these opinions differently from the way legislative policies would.

More Than Naysaying

The classic image of modern judicial review is that of the Court intervening to protect politically powerless minorities from hostile majorities. The Court does not so much "impose a policy" on the nation, as simply prevent the enforcement of an unjust policy on a relatively small group. For example, there was little direct effect on the life of the nation in the Court's telling West Virginia school boards that they could not punish Jehovah's Witnesses school children for not saluting the flag.[91] Likewise, telling states that they cannot prevent aliens from being lawyers[92] or telling Congress that it cannot treat widows and widowers differently in Social Security programs[93] does not seem to be all that immense an assertion of power.

In fact, however, judicial "naysaying" often can have very broad effects on national life, and judges have gone far beyond simply being naysayers in the contemporary exercise of judicial review.

In its obscenity decisions from 1959 to 1973, the Court acted as a naysayer, telling all levels of government that their power to suppress pornography was extremely limited. This made possible the tremendous expansion of pornography and the increasing legitimation of newer attitudes toward explicitness in sexual matters. While the Court decisions were only one factor in the creation and promotion of these attitudes (they were as much effects as causes), the legal protection they bestowed on the vehicles of such attitudes has had a significant effect on the atmosphere of American society, especially through the media. Material that was formerly limited to the underground or the margins of American public life is now casually accepted in its mainstream.[94] This may be a great victory for "honesty," according to judicial activists, but it is not the worth of the change that I am concerned with at the moment—it is simply the magnitude and the contributing role of judicial decisions that did no more than say "nay" to government regulation.

The Court's pre-1937 laissez-faire decisions were also "merely" naysaying; telling the government what it could and could not do in the realm of economic regulation to protect the economic rights of minorities; that is, not only the rights of businesses, but also the right of a District of Columbia woman elevator operator to work for less than minimum wage, perhaps rather than see the job eliminated.[95] The fact that the Court did not undertake, or command the legislature to undertake and fund, broad regulatory activity but simply said no to particular laws, did not mean that the effects of the decisions were narrow. When judges say no to a law, the implications of that decision depend upon the kind of law. Some naysaying by the Court will have few direct effects of any magnitude, but some will have a considerable impact. Saying no, then, can be equivalent in some cases to "imposing a policy" on the nation. Even if contemporary judicial review were merely naysaying, it would not necessarily be very limited.

However, contemporary judicial review has gone far beyond naysaying. Increasingly, courts have begun mandating certain programs or imposing affirmative obligations on government. In substance, if not in form, the Court has sometimes imposed an obligation on school districts to achieve racial balance in their schools by means incompatible with a neighborhood school policy, especially busing. Lower federal court judges have virtually taken over some districts to ensure proper racial balance.[96] The Court did not confine itself to striking down "crazy-quilt" apportionment and demanding a rational basis but mandated a particular kind of apportionment, "one-person, one-vote," and lower courts often devised the particular apportionment plans to be used.[97] Prison conditions have been declared "cruel and unusual punishment" and have thereby come under the direction of the courts,[98] and mental health institutions have likewise been subject to careful judicial scrutiny.[99] State systems of public school financing have been held to violate equal protection equivalents by state courts (although a campaign to achieve the same result under the Constitution fell one vote short of success in the Supreme Court), and a state court has even successfully ordered a legislature to institute an income tax to fund an alternative scheme.[100] Not only were certain kinds of police interrogation ruled to violate due process or the Fifth Amendment self-incrimination clause, but the Court provided specific language to be read to suspects in the form of the *Miranda* warnings.[101] Other decisions, which are negative in form, bear the marks of a detailed legislative plan for dealing with a broad social issue, as, for example, in the three-trimester division of pregnancy, with different standards for abortion in each trimester, contained in *Roe* v. *Wade*.[102]

The Court, then, is no longer simply a naysayer. It is able to impose many affirmative duties on government, and with its support lower courts have shown themselves quite willing to mandate and undertake the specific direction of important government policies. Whatever the limits on this judicial power, then—and there are limits of some kind on all power in American government—it is an immense power, and one subject to minimal control by ordinary majorities.

CONCLUDING ARGUMENTS: "GOOD RESULTS" AND "SPECIAL ABILITIES"

This section focuses on how defenders of judicial activism might respond to the critique of their arguments. We will address particularly the "good results" of judicial activism and the "special abilities" of judges.

Judicial activists obviously might defend the cases that are said to be bad results: busing, obscenity, abortion, and so on. Even where a "cost" of Court policies might be conceded, as with respect to criminal defendants' rights, activists may argue that the benefits outweigh the costs or that the costs can be reduced by other means that leave the Court's decisions intact. For example, the costs, in terms of fewer convictions of guilty persons due to extension of criminal rights, can be offset to some extent by improving the quality of police investigative work (more money, better training, new technology, etc.).

Most important, judicial activism's defenders argue that the net effect of increasing judicial power since 1937 has been beneficial. It is not pre-1937 activism or activism in general that they defend, but rather the libertarian and egalitarian activism of the modern era. The raison d'être of modern activism is the need to defend the integrity of the political process and the rights of discrete and insular minorities. The fact that an institutional power, such as that wielded by the modern Court, could be used badly (e.g., to protect powerful interests against the representatives of the people, as the Court did during the laissez-faire transitional era) is a factor to be weighed, but it is not conclusive. Even given the possibility that activism might once again be systematically put to purposes that would undermine its legitimacy, the benefits are substantial enough to justify the limited risk. The most likely "bad" scenario for judicial activists is the Court's return to self-restraint, leaving more matters to legislatures, where the activists can still wage a battle for their principles. From that standpoint, judicial activism is close to a no-lose situation for most of its contemporary defenders. If they succeed in maintaining it or extending judicial power, they benefit politically; if they do not succeed, they are no worse off than they would have been anyway.

Thus, the net effect of modern activism, even given some bad decisions, more than justifies its existence. When bad decisions are weighed against good decisions, and when the potential for good decisions is weighed against the potential for bad decisions, the balance favors modern judicial review.

The opponents of judicial activism come to a different conclusion, especially with regard to the potential abuse of the power. How many political evils have resulted from powers whose exercise seemed benign for relatively short periods, such as the fifty years or so of modern judicial review? How many of the good results of judicial review would have come about eventually through the normal operation of the political process, without the dangers of excessive judicial power?

And, in the final analysis, does the net potential of modern judicial review for good or ill differ significantly from that of an indirectly elected monarch with limited powers who could be checked by extraordinary majorities of a legislature? The main difference between the two would be the permanent suspicion about monarchical government inherent in the American political culture compared to the respect and trust for judges that originally derived from their association with the rule of law and that continues to survive despite the more tenuous links with that principle, perhaps in part because the average citizen knows so little about judicial power today.

This public confidence in the judges and their special abilities regarding the law and the Constitution is the mainstay of the modern Court's legitimacy. Part of this reputation is based on the fairly high level of personal integrity among federal judges, especially when compared to the notably less distinguished character of some legislators.[103] Their freedom from the "compromising" (in its many senses) character of political action, campaigns as well as policy-making, reinforces this reputation: individuals of no less integrity who act responsibly in the political process (that is, not as ideologues who posture moralistically) sometimes do not appear to have as much integrity. The legislative process is not the natural habitat of those who desire coherent, "principled" political action. American politics and legislative procedure tend to favor logrolling, expediency, and sensitivity to powerful interests. By defending unpopular minorities against hostile local majorities, the Court can increase its reputation for disinterested, principled action.

Moreover, even with modern caseloads, judges have the time and opportunity to reflect on broad constitutional issues, without the immediate tug of "the expedient" that legislators face. Not only is the opportunity available, but the public expects judges to live up to their peculiar responsibility for confronting and resolving constitutional issues. This responsibility is supported, even extended, by the norms of the legal profession, from whose ranks the justices are chosen. Defenders of the Court would argue that this profession is not characterized by ideological homogeneity, for it reflects the genuine pluralism of American intellectual life, including representation of many different political and social views.

Nor are judges' supposed "special disabilities" inherent in their role. If they lack special expertise in certain areas, they are provided with specialized information through the ordinary adversarial process and in special instances through "masters."[104] Judges can and do give weight to "practical" considerations, as they did following *Brown* v. *Board of Education* II, allowing the South time to desegregate.[105] Legal decisions can be and are modified in the light of experience, as the exclusionary rule has been limited, and may be limited further,[106] and as the Warren Court obscenity ruling in the *Fanny Hill* case was overturned.[107] The judicial process often makes "compromise and accommodation" of interests possible by preventing less powerful interests from simply being crushed or ignored in the ordinary political process, as with the rights of prisoners, not every legislator's favorite constituency. A casual notice of the number of settlements out of court and the pervasiveness of plea bargaining in the criminal justice system make clear the capacity of the courts to foster negotiation, compromise, and accommodation.

Critics who argue that the Court does not accommodate interests and engages in too much ad hoc adjudication cannot have it both ways. The very reason for the latter criticism is that the Court often does try very hard to come up with decisions that balance a variety of competing interests, rather than laying down a stark principle without regard for its impact on different interests or groups.

It is desirable to give greater weight to a plaintiff's concrete harms than to vague social interests. Too often nebulous social interests, such as the encouragement of patriotism in schoolchildren through required flag salutes have been given precedence over important individual rights, such as the conscientious religious rights of Jehovah's Witnesses not to perform actions they consider damnable.[108]

Again, supporters and opponents of judicial activism can agree that sometimes judicial action is characterized by such special weaknesses and that sometimes these tendencies can be successfully resisted. Its supporters, however, will be confident that the tendencies can be resisted and that judicial failures in these respects are outweighed by the benefits of broad judicial power. Activism's opponents are convinced that these special disabilities are inherent in the nature and form of judicial activity. To the extent that judges try to resist them, they get away from that nature, and those forms. For example, appointing a special master to make factual determinations seems more comparable to legislative action, such as relying on committee staff or securing expert testimony through hearings or interest group expertise, than to judicial action. The more judges look like legislators in their activity, the more difficult it is for them to claim special abilities deriving from the supposedly *judicial* character of their activity. The good that judges are able to accomplish is outweighed by the danger that this newly broadened power brings with it: the danger of incompetence, grandiose efforts to effect unattainable or excessively expensive results, and unjustifiable domination over popular majorities by judges on behalf of certain ideological views. The real "special ability" valued by supporters of judicial activism, its opponents might say, is the ability to impose a policy not supported by a majority or to prevent the execution of a policy supported by a majority. If this is supposedly done in the name of democratic "values," it is only because democratic "values" are understood so generally that everybody can consider their own beliefs and actions "democratic."

The final evaluation of such arguments is likely to involve balancing various strengths and weaknesses of the contending positions. Such a process can be quite difficult, because it is inherently a qualitative judgment; no quantitative methodology will take us very far in summing up the pros and cons. In evaluating results of judicial activism, for instance, how do you "weigh" the good done by *Brown* v. *Board of Education of Topeka* against the harm done by *Roe* v. *Wade* (assuming you consider those cases in that light)? Or how much weight should you accord the evils of "conservative" judicial activism in the first part of this century when weighing it against the good of post–1937 activism (again, assuming that is how you view those eras)?

Moreover, an important part of any argument will involve speculation as to what would have happened if things had been different. If there had been no judicial activism, how long would the South's legal, systematic racial discrimination have gone on? How significant were the economic and other effects of early twentieth-century "laissez-faire" decisions, compared to what would have happened in their absence? If the Warren Court had not handed down its decisions on criminal defendants' rights, would subsequent crime rates have been any lower? If the Court had never decided *Roe* v. *Wade*, would abortion rights have been broadened anyway, and how much, how quickly? If the Court had not upheld busing, would the comparative state of the educational achievement of minorities today and in the future be higher or lower?

And, of course, there is always the "prophetic" dimension of our decisions. We evaluate political arrangements to a great extent on what they have done in the past, but we must also consider what their "likely" future effects will be, which involves even broader conceptions of future developments and their implications. For example, our beliefs about the future of judicial power will reflect, at least in part, our beliefs about the future of the other branches of government: How are the legislative and executive branches changing? Will they be different? If so, how? All of these beliefs will be affected by our perceptions about the general direction of society in the future.

Difficult as such evaluations can be, they are an important part of our attempt to evaluate modern judicial activism. We must reflect on our perhaps unstated assumptions about such matters if we are to arrive at a coherent, persuasive understanding of the judiciary's role, especially in the Supreme Court.

CHAPTER FOUR

Democracy and the Indirect Effects of Judicial Review

U p to this point, we have been concentrating primarily on the direct impact of judicial review: What its immediate effects, or the sum of those immediate effects, are or are likely to be over time. This chapter, however, will focus on other, more indirect effects of judicial review.

UNDERMINING DEMOCRACY INDIRECTLY

James Bradley Thayer

James Bradley Thayer set forth the classic argument against the indirectly antidemocratic effects of judicial review in his 1893 *Harvard Law Review* article, "The Origin and Scope of the American Doctrine of Constitutional Law," and repeated it in his 1901 book on Chief Justice John Marshall.[1]

Thayer wrote during the upswing of laissez-faire judicial review, and in chapter 5 of his book on Marshall, he noted a number of effects arising from the increased exercise of judicial review. First, legislatures grow more and more accustomed to turning the subject of constitutional restraints over to the courts, falling insensibly "into the habit of assuming that whatever they can constitutionally do they may do."[2] Second, the people become more careless about whom they send to legislatures, confident that the "few wiser gentlemen on the bench are so ready to protect them against their more immediate representatives."[3] Third, the exercise of judicial review is

> always attended with a serious evil, namely, that the correction of legislative mistakes comes from the outside, and the people thus lose the political experience, and the moral education and stimulus that comes from fighting the question out in the ordinary way, and correcting their own errors.[4]

Even if striking down a bad law would save the country trouble and harm, still Thayer thought:

> the good which come[s] to the country and its people from the vigorous thinking that ha[s] to be done in the political debates that follow . . . , from the infiltration through every part of the population of sound ideas and sentiments, from the rousing into activity of opposite elements, the enlargement of ideas, the strengthening of moral fiber, and the growth of political experience that [comes] out of it all,—that all this far more than outweigh[s] any evil which ever flow[s] from the refusal of the court to interfere with the work of the legislature.[5]

Thus, he concludes:

> The tendency of a common and easy resort to this great function, now lamentably too common, is to dwarf the political capacity of the people, and to deaden its sense of moral responsibility.[6]

Alexis de Tocqueville

Alexis de Tocqueville is often cited as supporting the importance of judicial power.[7] With regard to the traditional understanding of judicial review as the enforcement of clear constitutional commands, Tocqueville would certainly be a strong proponent. An important aspect of *Democracy in America*, however, raises questions about whether he would be happy with the expansion of *modern* judicial power.

In the second volume of his work Tocqueville argues that the natural tendency of a modern democratic regime is to weaken the bonds between a man and his fellow citizens, confining the individual's concerns to himself and a narrow circle of friends.[8] This individualism is reinforced by the particularly strong desire for physical well-being in a democracy, which leads men to devote their energies primarily to the pursuit of their own comfort.[9]

Tocqueville sees in this tendency the possibility of a radically new kind of despotism—mild and soft, degrading without tormenting, all-embracing. The love of well-being, manifested in the preference for equality over liberty, may lead people to sacrifice political freedom for the "advantages" of this soft despotism, that is, the more certain attainment of "petty and paltry pleasures" achievable through "an immense and tutelary . . . absolute, minute, regular, provident, and mild" power.[10] In this despotism "the will of man is not shattered, but softened, bent, and guided," and the "nation is reduced to nothing better than a flock of timid and industrious animals, of which the government is the shepherd."[11]

How can this democratic tendency be thwarted? According to Tocqueville, one of the major antidotes in America is the political participation of the people in free institutions of government. This participation helps each person see the limits of his independence and the necessity of acting together with others. The problems of government with which he is faced cause him to look beyond his own narrow circle of concerns and to contribute to the public good, not for altruistic reasons, but from a refined and enlightened self-interest: a self-interest rightly understood. This makes the citizens capable of "great and real sacrifices to the public welfare" and "faithful support to one another."[12]

This public participation occurs especially on the local levels of government. It is necessary, Tocqueville says, "to infuse political life into each portion of the territory in order to multiply to an infinite extent opportunities of acting in concert for all the members of the community and to make them constantly feel their mutual dependence."[13]

Tocqueville is very clear-sighted about the results of popular participation in government, the costs as well as the benefits.

> It is uncontestable that the people frequently conduct public business badly; but it is impossible that the lower orders should take part in public business without extending the circle of their ideas and quitting the ordinary routine of their thoughts. . . .

> Democratic liberty is far from accomplishing all its projects with the skill of an adroit despotism . . . but in the end it produces more than any absolute government; if it does fewer things well, it does a greater number of things. . . .

Democracy does not give the people the most skillful government, but it produces what the ablest governments are frequently
unable to create: namely, an all-pervading and restless activity, a
superabundant force, and an energy which is inseparable from it and
which may, however unfavorable circumstances are, produce wonders. These are the true advantages of democracy.[14]

Tocqueville's position can be summed up in his statement that "elected
magistrates do not make the American democracy flourish; it flourishes
because the magistrates are elective."[15]

Tocqueville's position thus requires an observer of political affairs to
step back and view the regime in a broad perspective. More important, it
requires the great political virtue of moderation (even in virtue?): One must,
to some extent, observe the defects of government in a democracy and yet
withstand the strong "temptation" to remedy specific defects in certain ways
that prevent less immediate and tangible evils, but create more pervasive and
dangerous ones. Democracy must indulge the parental assumption that the
mistakes a child makes are the *necessary* price for the invaluable training
given only by experience. Thus, as Tocqueville says:

It would seem as if the rulers of our time sought only to use
men in order to make things great; I wish that they would try a little
more to make great men; that they would set less value on the work
and more upon the workman; that they would never forget that a
nation cannot long remain strong when every man belonging to it
is individually weak; and that no form or combination of social
polity has yet been devised to make an energetic people out of a
community of pusillanimous and enfeebled citizens.[16]

This is the underlying notion that is necessary to understand
Lincoln's claim that the purpose of democracy is "to elevate the condition
of men." That elevation consists not in providing people with goods and
services or "welfare," but in releasing their energies and developing their
capacities, and this occurs when the nation chooses "to lift artificial
weights from all shoulders . . . and to clear the paths of laudable pursuit
for all."[17]

It is precisely this concern for the work rather than the workman that
makes the extension of judicial power look dangerous. The power of even a
body of genuinely prudent judicial guardians would have to be greatly
restricted in a democracy, because the price of whatever good it could
mandate would be the loss of the people's experience of self-government.

Advocates of extended judicial power often base their arguments on the necessity of guaranteeing the conditions of democracy; for example, procedural conditions such as free speech or substantive conditions such as social equality, either for its own sake or to prevent gross political inequality. What these advocates fail to fathom is that the conditions of democracy ultimately rely on an informed public opinion that depends on political experience.[18] If a people never argue about free speech and its proper limits, for example, they will lose the sense of what free speech is, no matter how much the courts expound their views of it; and if a people have no political power to regulate and enforce free speech, they will have little incentive to discuss it.

The loss of political responsibility engendered by the extension of judicial power applies to legislatures, as Thayer notes. But it applies *a fortiori* to the people, and it is on the people that a democracy relies. A healthy democracy will not last for long if the government is only for the people and not of and by them as well. If there is a price to pay for this, and there surely is a significant one, it is a necessary price.

The danger to democracy occasioned by extended judicial power is surely more subtle than what most of the Court's contemporary critics are concerned with. That danger is reflected in a footnote to *Democracy in America*:

> It cannot be absolutely or generally affirmed that the greatest danger of the present age is license or tyranny, anarchy or despotism. Both are equally to be feared; and the one may proceed as easily as the other from one and the same cause: namely, that *general apathy* which is the consequence of individualism. It is because this apathy exists that the executive government, having mustered a few troops, is able to commit acts of oppression one day; and the next day a party which has mustered some thirty men in its ranks can also commit acts of oppression. Neither the one nor the other can establish anything which will last; and the causes which enable them to succeed easily prevent them from succeeding for long; they rise because nothing opposes them, and they sink because nothing supports them. The proper object, then, of our most strenuous resistance is far less either anarchy or despotism than that apathy which may almost indifferently beget either the one or the other.[19]

Even if the modern, expansive form of judicial review can be used to achieve some good, the loss of political education through self-government, which is the price of that good, may endanger the foundations of a free republic.

Finally, the major effect of Tocqueville's argument, which reinforces its application to modern judicial review, may be less the shift of power from legislature to judiciary than from state and local government to federal. The "constitutionalizing" of issues leads to their ultimate resolution by the Supreme Court, a branch of the national government. In most cases, the exercise of judicial review is aimed at state and local acts, not federal acts. This fact is especially important because frequent and extensive political participation is most possible in local government.[20] To the extent that local government is deprived of political power, there is less incentive for political participation by most of the citizenry.

DEFENSE OF JUDICIAL ACTIVISM

Is Thayer correct in arguing that modern judicial review makes legislatures less sensitive to constitutional issues and voters less careful about choosing legislators, and that the people lose the political education of fighting the issue out in the legislatures?

There is no question that legislatures are not as sensitive to constitutional issues as they once were. It is not at all clear why this is true and whether it is altogether undesirable. The decline in concern about constitutional issues may reflect not so much the indirect effects of modern judicial review as the nature of the most important contemporary political issues and the national-ization of American life.

The central political issues of the last century have been foreign affairs and the national economy—areas left almost entirely to the polit-ical branches by the Constitution and the modern Court. The one major constitutional principle implicated is federalism. But, a defender of judi-cial activism might argue, the decline of federalism in modern America[21] is less a function of judicial activity than of the nationalization of Amer-ican life: Modern transportation, communication, geographical mobility, and so on, have made Americans a single political community rather than a federation of quite different communities, as they were in 1787. If legislatures do not debate issues of federalism more, it is because their constituents do not feel strongly about these issues, not because the Supreme Court has taken those issues away from them. Although the Court may have had some indirect influence in diminishing popular concern about federalism through its "educative" role, the primary reason for this decreasing interest is that modern conditions—economic condi-tions, especially, and foreign affairs—have caused people to shift the locus of their primary political interest and expectations from the state to the national government.[22]

Nor is it clear that legislative inattention to constitutional issues is undesirable; it may reflect a certain healthiness of the regime. When have constitutional issues been most salient in legislative chambers? During the founding and up to the Civil War, questions such as Alexander Hamilton's financial program and Congress' implied powers, internal improvements, and slavery were central political questions. The legislative discussion of these issues reflected widespread controversy about the meaning of the Constitution in these matters. That controversy, however, was frequently dangerous to the peace and preservation of the regime. The controversies of the 1790s and the slavery question both involved what might be called "regime" questions; that is, questions about the very nature of the regime, its most important political principles.[23]

Widespread controversy about "regime" questions is a two-edged sword. There are beneficial effects, for thought, debate, and general concern over very important principles occur, often raising the level of public debate and calling forth great leaders. However, such controversy can also bring about dangerous political instability and even civil war, for what is at stake is fundamental and compromise is often impossible.

If constitutional issues are not salient, then, in legislatures or among the populace, perhaps that is grounds for satisfaction, not lamentation.[24] One of the rare instances in modern American politics when constitutional questions did become the center of legislative attention occurred in 1973, with the Watergate impeachment inquiry of a House Judiciary Committee subcommittee. There was something genuinely elevating in that experience—how often does one see representatives with copies of the *Federalist* in their pockets?—but on the whole, wouldn't the country have been better off if Watergate had never happened?

What would the effect on U.S. politics be if Congress and the state legislatures suddenly became the ultimate arbiters of questions concerning freedom of speech and religion, due process, and equal protection? Would they address themselves seriously to the constitutional issues? There are at least reasonable grounds to doubt whether the legislative process would encourage, or sometimes even permit, deliberation on such matters.[25]

If legislatures are "deliberate," in the sense of not acting quickly, how much do they genuinely "deliberate," in the sense of serious reflection and reasoned discussion? Courts usually have to give reasoned answers to litigants; legislatures can simply ignore those groups without significant political support, regardless of whether they have serious grounds to complain of unjust treatment. The contraction of modern judicial review would not guarantee any greater legislative attention to important constitutional questions.

Given the importance of the "nonconstitutional" questions that legislatures face, including most of the "bread-and-butter" and foreign affairs issues, it is hard to believe that voters are more careless about whom they send to the legislature simply because they have a trusted judiciary to protect them. Judicial activists today seem as concerned with getting good legislators as their opponents. After all, judicial activists do not argue that judges should decide everything: Foreign policy and most economic questions, indeed the vast majority of political issues, are still decided by legislatures.

There are more plausible grounds to ask whether there is a genuine loss of political education when judicial intervention in certain areas short-circuits legislative activity to attain the same result. Here too, however, the defenders of judicial activism would argue that the reverse is the case; that is, that judicial intervention may increase political participation and education.

First, recent reactions against Court decisions (e.g., Warren Court decisions and *Roe* v. *Wade*) suggest that this may occur. Besides the direct effects of protecting political rights (e.g., voting rights of blacks and the speech rights of unpopular minorities such as Communists and antiwar demonstrators in the 1960s),[26] Court decisions can *mobilize* political participation by putting on the political agenda issues that otherwise might not be there. For example, the effect of *Roe* v. *Wade*, one of the most controversial decisions of the modern Court, has been to mobilize the antiabortion movement. The movement is now far more extensive and active than it was in the pre-1973 period, when a few legislatures had started to "liberalize" abortion laws, and public opinion supporting traditional laws started getting "soft."[27]

This mobilization occurred precisely because there *are* usable checks on Court power that make it politically vulnerable. The appointment power is the primary check, but others such as cutting off Court jurisdiction are available as well.

Second, judicial review from the very beginning has been understood to be profoundly *educative*. This was one of James Madison's most important arguments for the Bill of Rights.[28] John Marshall's judicial career was a potent example of this capacity for education. His defenses of the Constitution's principles against unjustifiable constriction of federal power or legislative impairment of contractual obligations had a deep impact on American political life.

In the modern era, the Court has helped bring about a fundamental change in the nation's race relations. The racism implicit in pre–*Brown* v. *Board of Education* segregation has not been eliminated from American life, but it is no longer publicly defensible as it once was, and the Court clearly deserves a significant portion of the credit for this.[29]

The very salience of the Bill of Rights as a symbol of individual liberties is testimony to the success of the modern Court in educating the citizenry in the basic principles of liberal democracy. Studies of political culture show that the emphasis on rights in American life is quite distinctive.[30] And who do Americans see as representative of our commitment to rights? The Supreme Court. The point here is not whether Americans *should* single out the Supreme Court. Even if one were to object that this commitment is symbolized better by other facets of American government, that would still leave the question, who represents the American commitment to rights? And if Americans look to the Supreme Court, as a defender of the Court could argue, that would demonstrate the Court's significant, positive educative impact in the area of rights.

Effects such as these are the grounds for Eugene Rostow's argument (in a seminal 1952 article on the democratic character of judicial review) that the Court is a "vital national seminar." Its decisions often stimulate rather than dampen public debate and thereby contribute to the political education of the citizenry. The "work of the Court can have, and when wisely exercised does have, the effect not of inhibiting but of releasing and encouraging the dominantly democratic forces of American life."[31] Given the Court's ability to put on the nation's political agenda questions that legislators have been unwilling or unable to consider, this political education is even more effective in some ways than the ordinary political process described by Thayer. At the very least, it is a valuable supplement to that process.

RENEWED CRITICISM

An opponent of judicial activism would deny that legislative consideration of constitutional issues necessarily signals such uncertainty about basic principles to occasion substantial political instability. If there are deep divisions about essential constitutional issues, instability may occur, of course, as with slavery. But the "ordinary" constitutional questions will not be so dangerous. Part of the problem is the modern incapacity to see some genuine constitutional questions. Is a particular program really justified as a "necessary and proper" law for carrying into effect a power of the national government? Marshall holds out the possibility that in an extreme case the Court might strike down a law, should "Congress, under the pretext of executing its powers, pass laws for the accomplishment of objects not entrusted to the government."[32] But many laws that fall short of a clear violation might raise constitutional questions, which a legislator could consider even if a judge should not. The same is true with respect to the commerce clause, taxing and spending power, separation of powers, and the just compensation or takings clause.

These questions often involve questions of federalism. But the "nationalization" of American life does not make federalism irrelevant. First, the nationalization is only partial, as a comparison of different regional and political cultures shows.[33] Second, even with nationalization, Justice Louis Brandeis's classic argument for using states as laboratories to experiment with different solutions to complex social problems retains its great force.[34] As a matter of fact, states often devise different approaches to the same problem, and these differences are precisely the object of judicial activists' efforts, for they believe that only one of a variety of possible solutions is acceptable and ought to be mandated by judges. Third, even if federalism has become outmoded, the proper way to deal with it would be amendment, so that the issue is dealt with directly and coherently and not merely through the tangential effects of many different cases. If the response to this point is that an amendment is too difficult to secure, then this suggests that a large number of Americans take federalism more seriously than most judicial activists do. The fact that many constitutional questions arising before legislatures involve federalism cannot be dismissed on the grounds of judicial activists' distaste for that principle.

That other constitutional questions—especially those involving civil liberties and equality—do not arise more frequently in legislatures may reflect the nature of the contemporary political and legislative process, but it may also reflect precisely what Thayer was worried about—the habit Americans have fallen into of considering constitutional questions as judicial questions. We do not know what the case would be if modern judicial review had not been in practice for the past century or so. Can we assume that had the judicial arena been available only for questions of clear constitutional rights, the forces that have been so effective in raising these questions in the judicial arena would have been unable to do so in the political process?[35] It would perhaps be worthwhile recalling here Justice Holmes's admonition against confusing the familiar with the inevitable. If the Supreme Court were abolished today, would the ACLU and NAACP, for example, be politically powerless? They would certainly lose some battles that they might have won in court, but given the typical political complexion of Congress they would certainly win quite a few too.[36]

There is no reason to assume that such groups could not put questions on the legislative agenda, or that—in the absence of a judicial power that makes efforts seem unnecessary or fruitless—they would not be deliberated upon in the legislature's normal way (i.e., through committees, and subject to the body's willingness to accept their proposals). No one will pretend that legislative deliberation is always satisfactory, but its results, especially keeping in mind some pretty egregious judicial blunders, are not that bad either.[37]

No one will doubt that judicial decisions have their own special educative power. But does this response adequately address Thayer's concerns? There are different kinds of political education, and one cannot lightly assume that one kind automatically substitutes for another. What kind of education was Thayer talking about? Not simply "giving the people the right answer" and thereby improving the state of society. Intelligent defense and explication of constitutional principles are very desirable, but Thayer points out that other things, along the lines suggested by Tocqueville, are necessary too.

The education involved in battling out a question in the legislature is important in terms of the effects of the process on those involved in it, as well as the result. Individuals who become actively involved in campaigns and building political support for an issue before the legislature and those who follow the struggle in the legislature and in campaigns gain a depth of view and experience that goes beyond education "from the outside." For example, if questions involving freedom of speech had to be fought out in legislatures instead of being consigned by modern habit to the courts, perhaps public understanding of that principle would be improved.[38] As it is, political scientists frequently argue that while attachment to freedom of speech as a general principle is universal in America, the implications of it—accepting the rights of unpopular minorities to free speech—are often rejected.[39] Perhaps Americans are "taught" too much about freedom of speech rather than "learning about it" themselves. *How much* this reflects the preemption of legislative consideration of civil liberties by judicial domination in such issues is, of course, impossible to say.

If Thayer's argument has weight, judicial protection of some political principles may actually contribute to their downfall. Think of Thayer's own audience, for example: individuals who advocated using judicial power to strike down economic regulation in order to protect property rights. When the issue was left to the ordinary political process, after 1937, they lost decisively. Thayer might have observed that if the issue had been fought in the legislatures rather than in the courts from the beginning, the educative process of consideration and debate might have resulted in a more balanced appreciation of the need to protect property rights to some extent, even as they were being regulated, instead of leaving them with virtually no judicial protection at all, as occurred after 1937 (until the the contract and takings clauses were partially resurrected much later). Robert McCloskey pointed out that the extreme protection of property rights before 1937 may help to account for the extreme abdication that followed: One extreme bred another.[40]

If Court decisions can mobilize groups and thereby increase political participation, they can alienate groups as well. The long-term effect of *Roe* v. *Wade* is yet to be determined. Opposition to it has been possible because of concrete short-term goals that were left open, especially opposition to public funding of abortion, which the Court left to the political process in *Harris* v. *McRae*.[41] Had the political process been short-circuited more completely, so that antiabortion forces were left with only the long-term goal of overturning the decision, the ultimate effect might have been a substantial alienation of a large group of people from the American political process.[42]

Finally, the educative role of the Supreme Court cited by judicial activists in defense against Thayer's argument is a source of other, more substantive problems, which brings us back to the arguments of previous chapters. There is no question that the Court has an educative role, but what purposes should it be used for? One of the most significant problems with modern judicial review is that it has become detached from the Constitution. Providing education in the principles of the Constitution is clearly a legitimate role for the Court. But what about the legitimacy of the Court that espouses its own principles, perhaps principles that are contrary to the Constitution's? The modern Court has had a profound educative influence in its advocacy of libertarian and egalitarian principles that are quite contrary to the Constitution. For example, the notion of political liberty in First Amendment cases, perhaps especially regarding seditious speech and obscenity, and the notion of political equality embraced in the reapportionment decisions are demonstrably contrary to the original intent.[43] The Court has adopted certain modern ideological propensities of the legal profession, which reflect developments in modern philosophy that are influential among intellectual elites, even though these tendencies do not always concur with the majority of the American people and with the Constitution. The result has been an undermining of constitutional principles and a shift in the nature of the regime.

CONCLUSION

The answers that defenders of judicial activism would give to these arguments should be pretty clear from earlier discussions: the shortcomings of the amendment process, the superiority of the judicial process to the legislative process in questions of civil liberties, and, above all, the simple fact that the overall results of the Court's efforts to expand liberty and equality have been more beneficial than harmful. Opponents of judicial activism reach the opposite conclusion, they would say, only because they are excessively optimistic about what would have happened in the absence of judicial intervention.

The American political experience of the last ninety years demonstrates (they would argue) that judicial intervention in certain areas does not undermine the springs of political activity in our society. In many cases, in fact, judges have brought about or stimulated political activity, especially by unblocking the channels of political change. This has been accomplished in some cases by expanding broadly "procedural" rights, such as voting and free speech. And in other, substantive areas, justices have helped articulate emerging rights more clearly and facilitated their substitution for outdated legislation that no longer commanded genuine majority support. On the whole, then, judicial activism has more often been a stimulus to political activity than an obstacle.

CHAPTER FIVE

Conclusion

The dialectic on judicial activism of the preceding chapters shows that there are obviously strengths and weaknesses on both sides of the issue. The arguments we have looked at constitute the "building blocks" of cases for and against judicial activism. These arguments can be put together in various combinations, leading to different conclusions about how judicial power ought to be exercised. The result is the variety of contending "theories of judicial review" that occupy the literature on the subject today.

As I noted at the beginning of the book, this dialectic cannot be reduced to an "either/or" question, either for judicial activism or against it. There is a broad continuum of positions, ranging from opposition to all judicial activism in principle to advocacy of virtually unfettered judicial discretion. In fact, the spectrum could be expanded by raising the question of the desirability of judicial review itself, even of a "constitutional" variety, although that would go beyond the scope of this book. In between these extremes are many more qualified positions that would accept judicial activism under some circumstances but not others. Most major theories of judicial review insist that *some* limits be set on judicial power, the specific limits varying from theory to theory.

Since throughout most of this book we have entertained arguments "for" and "against" judicial activism, it might be worthwhile to give a simple example of an intermediate position.

A CASE FOR MODERATE
JUDICIAL ACTIVISM

"Moderate" judicial activism (not to be confused with the "moderate" judicial *review* of the traditional era described in the Introduction) would share the essential features of modern forms of judicial power; that is, it would be derived from sources outside the specific content of the Constitution and therefore be fundamentally legislative in character, but it could be limited in a number of ways. First, moderate judicial activism could limit itself to certain functions, such as protecting the integrity of the political process, with a special sensitivity to voting rights and freedom of speech. The last part of the *Carolene Products* rationale—the protection of discrete and insular minorities—might also be a useful but limited function if the minorities were confined to those with some kind of constitutional status, such as religious minorities (from the First Amendment), racial minorities (from the Thirteenth, Fourteenth, and Fifteenth Amendments), criminal defendants (from a number of Bill of Rights guarantees), and perhaps certain property owners (from the contract clause). The practical implication of these limits (i.e., the proof that they are a limit) is that some activist decisions, such as in the area of abortion and the attempted use of *Roe* v. *Wade* as a precedent for homosexual rights cases, would be ruled out.[1]

Second, a moderate form of judicial activism might be cautious in the manner of exercising this power in performing such functions. For example, it might try to break up political impasses, as *Baker* v. *Carr* opened the way for reapportionment, but it might accept a variety of remedies, unlike the "rigid" one-person, one-vote remedy for malapportionment in *Reynolds* v. *Sims*. Having intervened to put certain political or social reforms on the national agenda, moderate judicial activism might then defer to the ordinary political process for the specific resolution of such problems.[2] Or it might strike down illegitimate discrimination, as *Brown* v. *Board of Education of Topeka* did, but unlike *Brown* II, and later cases such as *Green* v. *County School Board* and *Swann* v. *Charlotte-Mecklenberg*, it could simply order that henceforth state action must be racially neutral, forgoing any attempt to impose particular remedies for establishing social equality.

Another form of limited activism could employ what Louis Lusky called "tentative" judicial review, in which the Court strikes down laws in such a way that the legislature is free to pass a similar law if it chooses to.[3] For example, when the Court strikes down state legislation on the grounds that it burdens interstate commerce, it effectively puts the ball in Congress's court, since Congress is free to authorize such state legislation. Similarly, the Court might accept congressional statutes authorizing certain state practices in the criminal justice area, pursuant to its power under Section 5 of the Fourteenth Amendment, that it has struck down when based only on state legislation. Or another form of limited activsm could be the Court's striking down of old legislation allegedly based on religious taboos such as abortion or obscenity laws, leaving open the possibility of new legislation that is clearly based on other grounds.[4]

By moderating judicial activism through some combination of limits on the subject matter, the scope of remedies, or the definitiveness of Court action, it might be possible to construct a stronger case for judicial activism by limiting opportunities for abusing it.

The Case Against Moderate Judicial Activism

Even this case for more moderate judicial activism, however, appears unpersuasive to traditionalists. First, beware the siren song of "moderation." Rarely do people like to consider themselves "extremist," which is presumably the opposite of moderation; it is almost always more comfortable to be in the middle. But whether being "moderate" is desirable depends entirely on the particular spectrum and its extremes.

Second, a "moderate" position cannot be created simply with words. It would be meaningless to be a moderate judicial activist in the sense of only favoring activism when it has good results. It would be necessary not only to define the substantive content of what would be considered good results, but also to show how to obtain those good results from a given set of political arrangements.

Most judicial activists, even those who advocate rather extensive judicial power, probably consider themselves "moderate." The more difficult questions would be whether a given understanding of moderation is adequate, and how its limits could be enforced in practice.

Special "functions" such as those specified in the *Carolene Products* footnote can be used to justify an enormous range of powers.[5] The notion of minority rights in particular is quite malleable. With a little imagination, most groups that lose in the legislature and have some strong principles as the basis of their position can claim some form of inappropriate discrimination.

A good example of the elasticity of such categories is John Hart Ely's "representation-reinforcing judicial review," which is based on a rejection of broad "fundamental rights" judicial review. Court decisions ought to be justified in terms of the more procedural value of opening clogged political channels. But "representation" turns out to be a very elastic concept. Groups are denied representation, for instance, if they are denied equal concern and respect when legislators operate on the basis of inaccurate stereotypes that flatter the majority at the expense of a minority.[6]

Even an "obvious" category for protection such as "political rights," can be viewed in extremely latitudinarian terms. One could start from such obvious categories of freedom of speech as political discussion and debate, and then move to broad artistic and cultural concerns, and then to self-expression and entertainment, and finally arrive at the conclusion that freedom of "speech" protects nude dancing in bars.[7]

Finally, too much injustice or wrong can be legislated by judges in the name of perfectly good intentions about preserving political and minority rights. Even a judicial activism restricted to protecting a limited range of rights could do considerable damage.

The general admonition to be cautious in the exercise of broad judicial power sounds nice, but such vague generalities are unlikely to be very effective in practice. Judicial activists do not think they are using their power lightly, but they argue that extreme circumstances—different forms of gross injustice, and legislative inactivity or positive sponsorship of the evil—have "forced" them to act. And when they act, they are willing to do what is necessary to eliminate the injustice, which means that abstract limits on judges' remedial powers are likely to fall before the demands of justice. For example, judicial activists favor broad remedies in school desegregation cases because they are convinced that these remedies are the only way to achieve their goal of racial equality. To say that only the "necessary" remedies should be used would be an illusory limit on judicial activism.

Moderate judicial activists would respond that they should not be held accountable for abuses of their arguments. Just because some "extremists" might extend their arguments unjustifiably, as in the nude-dancing example, is no reason to reject the sound core of the argument. And in principle some workable limits on judicial remedial powers could be formulated, since moderate activists recognize that sometimes the potential abuse of expansive remedial powers outweighs the abuses that are being challenged.

But this response ignores the practical difficulty of gaining agreement on such limits. The recognition that *Marbury* v. *Madison* no longer provides an adequate theoretical foundation for judicial review has spawned a cottage industry that devises "theories of judicial review" in law reviews and legal scholarship. And yet rather than promoting greater agreement on what should be done, these theories seem to produce more grist for law review articles and a greater supply of sources to cite in court opinions. That should not be surprising. Once the definition of the scope of judicial review is no longer attached to the Constitution or is attached in a way that allows such great latitude in interpretation, then judicial review can be redefined in myriad ways, with little agreement on which way should be authoritative.[8]

It is tempting to support tentative judicial review, since it seems to allow judicial activism to right certain kinds of wrongs *and* the possibility of legislative overruling of judicial acts. The practical effect is to give the benefit of doubt to claims of liberty against the claims of the status quo. The essential question is who will shoulder the burden of overcoming legislative inertia and checks. If activists think that anticontraceptive or antisodomy laws are really outdated relics of past religious and social taboos, should they have to overcome the obstacles to repealing them (since obstacles do exist, even if majority sentiment has changed)? Or should judges strike down such laws, thereby placing the burden on the laws' supporters to get them passed again? When seen in those terms, there is a striking similarity between this approach and Thomas Jefferson's suggestion that laws automatically lose their force after a set time on the grounds that the "earth belongs to the living."[9] The question then becomes "Why should only laws that the judges consider outdated be reversible?" Those who would be happy to see anticontraceptive or antisodomy laws judicially repealed ought to ask themselves whether minimum wage laws and various kinds of business regulation might not be seen in a similar light by more conservative judges, as relics of a more benighted era.

Moreover, unless the Court were to explicitly invite the legislature to repass the law if it wished and to promise to uphold it—a dubious possibility[10]—the inertia and checks would be magnified by the significant doubt as to whether the Court really would uphold it if it were passed again. Legislative time and resources, including the necessity of taking a stand that will make enemies, are precious commodities, and there is a natural reluctance to expend them, when in the final analysis it might be a waste of time.

Moderate judicial activism, then, is subject to criticism on the grounds that there is still too much room for judicial discretion and that theoretical limits on the judges could probably not be successfully and consistently enforced.

A FINAL WORD

The Founders of American government did not consider human nature simply and irremediably depraved, but they were profoundly convinced that human beings—all human beings—could not be trusted with excessive power.[11] "Excessive" power is an elastic concept, but it involves a prudent weighing of the need for the power and the alternative ways of providing for it, taking into consideration the possibility of providing effective checks. In this balancing process, judges must be included as well, for they too are subject to human weaknesses.

The Founders clearly did not rely on the judiciary as their primary institutional mechanism for protecting rights.[12] Rights were to be protected especially by the ordinary democratic process, emphasizing the principle of majority rule and the moderating effects of a multiplicity of interests in an extended republic. Courts were to be an auxiliary precaution, protecting a limited number of specified constitutional rights. The limited character of this power helps to explain why Alexander Hamilton calls the judicial branch "the least dangerous" branch. In *The Federalist,* No. 81 he inferred that the judiciary would not usurp legislative authority "from the general nature of the judicial power; from the objects to which it relates; from the manner in which it is exercised; from its comparative weakness, and from its total incapacity to support its usurpations by force."[13] What Hamilton had in mind was especially the predominantly "private law" character of judicial power. Judicial power existed primarily to resolve disputes between the government and individuals or between individuals according to law. The power of judicial review, the "public law" function, arose incidentally and infrequently out of its normal function of deciding cases.[14]

As long as judges conformed to this understanding of judicial power, the generally accepted understanding in the founding,[15] they could cause harm by particular bad decisions but would not upset "the order of the political system," as noted in *The Federalist,* No. 81. The notion of a very limited judicial power enabled it to be vested with great independence, without violating the general rule of the Founders that power must be effectively checked.

As we have seen, however, that traditional limited notion of judicial power has given way to a quite different modern notion, which exalts the judges' public law function. The decline of the standing doctrine, the expansion of declaratory judgments and class action suits, the development of an extensive armory of remedial powers, and the general acceptance within the legal profession of the notion that judicial power, even outside the common law, is fundamentally legislative have transformed judicial power and eliminated many of the factors that Hamilton and the other Founders had confidently relied on to keep judges' power properly limited.[16]

From the standpoint of the political philosophy of the founding, a response to this expansion of judicial power could take two forms. First, the transformation of judicial power could be accepted, with a call for an appropriate transformation of the checks on it. For example, the courts' increased power might be balanced by new checks, such as election of judges, limited tenure (perhaps ten years), or requirement for an extraordinary majority (six or seven votes) to strike down laws.

But there would be serious objections to this approach on several grounds. First, the new checks would require constitutional amendment, and their political practicability and prudence would be suspect. Second, and more important, such an approach would, in effect, constitute an acceptance of judicial legislative power by conferring legitimacy on it and might stimulate more judicial policymaking.

Another variation of this approach would be the use of already existing checks, such as impeachment and control of the size and jurisdiction of courts, in a new or transformed manner. Rather than reserving these checks, according to constitutional custom, for deliberate usurpations or for technical purposes, they could be employed for broader "constitutionally partisan" purposes.[17] This variation, however, might also be regarded as objectionable, even apart from the political difficulty of impeachment, which requires a two-thirds Senate vote, because it would require opponents of judicial activism to engage in a tactic, manipulation of constitutional powers for purposes not envisioned by the Founders, that is one of the problems they wish to attack. Moreover, this approach would also seem to confer legitimacy on judicial policymaking.

The second response to the expansion of judicial power would be to advocate a return to the older, more limited form of judicial power. This is a long-term, distinctly uphill battle of ideas, especially within the legal profession, because, among other reasons, it involves an attempt to persuade lawyers to adopt a view of judicial power that would lessen their own power.

History has shown that such changes are possible, however. Justice Oliver Wendell Holmes, Jr., won two such battles. In the more immediately political realm, his dissents in cases striking down economic regulation became "the voice of a new dispensation," as Justice Cardozo called it.[18] For thirty years Holmes led his forces in the wilderness, but he did not live to see the promised land. Nonetheless, the overthrow of economic due process came in 1937, shortly after his death, and was as total as he could have hoped for.

Holmes also won another battle in the realm of legal ideas, leading the forces of legal realism to victory and bequeathing to subsequent generations of American lawyers an occupational conviction that judges not only are not, but cannot be, the "mere" mouthpieces of the law.[19] His victory was hardly less complete in this matter, though there are more or less moderate forms of legal realism. In both cases, Holmes started his effort in what must have seemed very difficult circumstances, but they were no more difficult than the situations facing opponents of judicial activism today. If the latter effort to establish a legislative conception of law coincided with the underlying interests of lawyers in expanding their own powers, still the battle to eliminate review of economic regulation involved giving up power: Ideas overcame occupational self-interest.

Restoring the traditional understanding of judicial power would not be easy. Not the least of the difficulties would be how traditionalists would treat the large number of currently controlling precedents that are not rooted in the Constitution. The traditional approach would not automatically demand that every precedent based on weak constitutional logic be overturned. In 1815 James Madison, for example, signed into law a bill establishing a bank of the United States, although he had led the congressional fight against Alexander Hamilton's original proposal, on the grounds that Congress had no such power. Madison had not changed his view of the abstract merits of the constitutional arguments, he wrote, but simply adhered to his long-held view that "a course of authoritative expositions sufficiently deliberate, uniform, and settled, was an evidence of the public will necessarily overruling individual opinions," although there might be exceptions to this principle, "cases . . . which transcend all authority of precedents."[20] How much of modern constitutional law, so much of which is not rooted in a fair reading of the document, should be maintained as precedent would not be a simple question for traditionalists to answer.

If the traditional position has some difficult questions to face, and if short-term political forces make its return unlikely, nonetheless it does have one great untapped resource: the sharp contrast between the still-prevalent popular impression that judges ought to, and for the most part do, interpret law rather than make it—despite occasional "abuses"—and the dominant, but increasingly challenged, assumption within the legal profession that judges inevitably do, and should, make law.[21] If ordinary citizens come to see more clearly how lawyers and judges understand judicial power, then the foundations of modern judicial power could become shaky. This may be the major reason that courts are not explicit about the generally "legislative" character of modern judicial power. Combined with certain circumstances, e.g., other egregious decisions such as *Roe* v. *Wade*, declining legitimacy might at some point induce the legal profession and the nation to examine more seriously the question of the nature and proper scope of judicial power. Indeed, such a reexamination has already begun. Out of this reexamination, opponents of judicial activism can legitimately hope for the reestablishment of a balance of power among the different parts of our political system that is more in line with the prudence of the Founders of the American constitutional system.

NOTES

Preface

1. Thus, it assumes that *interpretation*, as I use the term in a stricter sense than is prevalent in legal scholarship today, is possible. While that is an important assumption, and one that may be unsatisfactory to some, a defense of it would divert the argument of this book too much. For the time being, see Wolfe, *The Rise of Modern Judicial Review* (New York: Basic Books, 1986). I hope to deal with that issue at greater length on other occasions.
2. Bickel, *The Least Dangerous Branch* (Indianapolis: Bobbs-Merrill, 1962), chapt. 1.
3. Some of the most notable new theories include John Hart Ely, *Democracy and Distrust* (Cambridge: Harvard University Press, 1980); Dworkin, *Taking Rights Seriously* (Cambridge: Harvard University Press, 1977), especially chapt. 5; and Perry, *The Constitution, the Courts and Human Rights* (New Haven: Yale University Press, 1982), and *Morality, Politics, and Law* (New York: Oxford University Press, 1988).

Among "original intention" legal scholars, the most prominent critics of this development have been Berger, *Government by Judiciary* (Cambridge: Harvard University Press, 1977); and Bork, *The Tempting of America* (New York: Free Press, 1990). Political science critics have included Berns, *The First Amendment and the Future of American Democracy* (New York: Basic Books, 1976); McDowell, *Equity and the Constitution* (Chicago: University of Chicago Press, 1982), and *Curbing the Courts* (Baton Rouge: Louisiana State University Press, 1988); and Rabkin, *Judicial Compulsions* (New York: Basic Books, 1989).

Another important development in legal scholarship during the 1970s and 1980s was the emergence of the Critical Legal Studies school, which attacked mainstream liberal theorizing from the left, denying the possibility of rule by legal principles and opting for a frankly political approach to all law. See, for example, Mark Tushnet, *Red, White, and Blue* (Cambridge: Harvard University Press, 1988). This radical critique, although important, cannot be integrated into this kind of dialectical discussion. and so must be left for another day.

4. Mill, *On Liberty* (Baltimore: Penguin, 1974), chapt. 2.
5. A fine example is Choper's *Judicial Review and the National Political Process* (Chicago: University of Chicago Press, 1980), a book whose conclusions I frequently disagree with, but one that I highly regard for its efforts to canvass both sides of important questions. The first chapter, "The Supreme Court and the Political Branches: Democratic Theory and Practice," is particularly impressive.

Introduction

1. Much of this section draws on several essays in Halpern and Lamb's very useful collection, *Supreme Court Activism and Restraint* (Lexington, Mass.: Lexington Press, 1982), especially Lamb, "Judicial Restraint on the Supreme Court," Schick, "Judicial Activism on the Supreme Court," and Canon, "A Framework for the Analysis of Judicial Activism."
2. Note particularly the scholarly debate, which can be traced back to J. Allen Smith's *The Spirit of American Government* (New York: Macmillan, 1907) and Beard's *An Economic Interpretation of the Constitution* (New York: Macmillan, 1913), with their contentions that the Founders were fundamentally representatives of commercial wealth and deliberately skewed the Constitution in a nondemocratic direction.

3. Madison, *The Federalist*, No. 51, ed. Garry Wills (New York: Bantam, 1982), p. 262

4. de Tocqueville, *Democracy in America*, vol. I, ed. Phillips Bradley (New York: Random House, Vintage, 1945), pp. 269–270

5. Madison, *The Federalist*, No. 51, pp. 261

6. Madison, *The Federalist*, No. 51, p. 261, 262

7. Madison, *The Federalist*, No. 51, p. 264

8. Madison, *The Federalist*, Nos. 10 and 51, pp. 49 and 265

9. Madison, *The Federalist*, No. 78, p. 397

10. Madison, *The Federalist*, No. 78, p. 397. The classic discussion of separation of powers, contained in *Federalist*, No. 51, does not mention the power of judicial review. (This reflects the fact that Madison did not accept the notion of judicial review as we usually think of it but rather embraced the more limited doctrine of coordinate or departmental review.) Because judicial review was formulated almost more as a legal doctrine than as a political one, one must be cautious about simply lumping the power of judicial review with other factors in discussions of checks and balances and separation of powers, an approach favored by John Agresto in his intelligent and interesting book, *The Supreme Court and Constitutional Democracy* (Ithaca, N.Y.: Cornell University Press, 1984).

11. For a developed presentation of this thesis, see Wolfe, *The Rise of Modern Judicial Review: From Constitutional Interpretation to Judge-Made Law* (New York: Basic Books, 1986).

12. For a different view, see H. Jefferson Powell, "Consensus and Objectivity in Early Constitutional Interpretation: An Unproven Thesis," *Texas Law Review* 65 (1987): 859. A key question is whether the very different applications of rules of interpretation, including different ideas as to the "nature" of our constitutional government, espoused by Alexander Hamilton and Thomas Jefferson, demonstrate that the Founders disagreed on the "fundamental" principles of constitutional interpretation itself.

13. It is worth stressing how subordinate such evidence was, especially in light of contemporary work that stresses extrinsic sources of intent; the most influential work is Berger, *Government by Judiciary: The Transformation of the Fourteenth Amendment* (Cambridge: Harvard University Press, 1977). The framers stressed that the fair reading of the document took precedence, and they tended to strongly downplay extrinsic sources of intention. For example, in the debate over the national bank, Alexander Hamilton argued, with respect to a proposition discussed at the Constitutional Convention, that "whatever may have been

the nature of the proposition, or the reasons for rejecting it, it concludes nothing with respect to the real merits of the question . . . whatever the intentions of the framers of the Constitution or of a law, that intention is to be sought for in the instrument itself, according to the usual and established rules of construction." (Henry Cabot Lodge, ed., *The Works of Alexander Hamilton* [New York: Putnam & Sons, 1904], 3, p. 463).

Hamilton's views on this issue were echoed in early constitutional debates by others such as James Madison. For a more extensive discussion of this issue, see Wolfe, "Constitutional Interpretation in the American Founding" (Ph.D. diss., Boston College, 1978). For a good contemporary overstatement of this point, see Powell, "The Original Understanding of Original Intention," *Harvard Law Review* 98 (1985): 885.

14. In response to the possibility that Section 9 could be construed to apply to both national and state governments, one can point out that some of the limitations of Section 9 are repeated in section 10 (e.g., the prohibition of ex post facto laws), and therefore Section 9's limits do not appear to apply to the states; otherwise the same limits need not have been repeated in Section 10).

15. This does not mean that there were no constitutional provisions that were unclear. Early interpreters would not have denied this possibility. The "meaning" of the Constitution in such cases was more a question of limiting the possible readings than of finding the sole legitimate reading. Interpretation resulted in the conclusion that several readings were plausible, and it ended at that point.

16. Madison, *The Federalist*, No. 78, p. 395; *Marbury* v. *Madison*, 1 Cranch 177

17. *Eakin* v. *Raub*, 12 Serg. & Rawle (Pa.) 330

18. For examples of early attempts to rein in the Court, see Warren, *The Supreme Court in U.S. History* (Boston: Little, Brown, 1926).

19. James Bradley Thayer calls legislative deference a "rule of administration" in his classic article, "The Origin and Scope of the American Doctrine of Constitutional Law," *Harvard Law Review* 7 (1893): 123.

20. No one claims that this principle was always followed in practice. People of every political stripe could point to some cases where they believe it was violated. But there is a considerable difference between negating a theoretical position or an ideal by falling short of it in some cases and denying it in principle and setting up another theoretical norm in its place. Of course, if the ideal were consistently negated in practice by those who espoused it seriously, one would have to wonder whether it

was a practicable ideal. The exact extent to which legislative deference as I have described it was really practiced in early American history is one of the more serious questions critics can raise about the adequacy of the traditional theory of judicial review.

21. *Luther* v. *Borden* 7 Howard 1 (1849).

22. But see Berger's argument to the contrary in his *Impeachment: The Constitutional Problems* (Cambridge: Harvard University Press, 1973).

23. Alexander Hamilton states the power more strongly in *The Federalist,* No. 78. John Marshall focuses on whether a court should treat a legislative act as controlling the court even when the Constitution prescribes a different rule. Hamilton is more expansive in asserting that "the courts were designed to be an intermediate body between the people and the legislature, in order, among other things, to keep the latter within the limits assigned to their authority" (*The Federalist,* No. 78, p. 395).

24. *Dred Scott* v. *Sandford,* 19 How. 393. Speech on the *Dred Scott* decision in Springfield 26 June 1857, in *The Political Thought of Abraham Lincoln,* ed. Richard Current (New York: Bobbs-Merrill, 1967), pp. 175–176.

25. *Osborn* v. *Bank of United States,* 9 Wheaton 738, 866 (1924). Cf. Cardozo, *The Nature of the Judicial Process* (New Haven: Yale University Press, 1921), p. 169.

26. And part of the meaning is that the Constitution says nothing about certain issues. To say that the Constitution says something when it says nothing is as much a misinterpretation as to say that it means *A* when it means *B.* This is important because some legal commentators argue that there is a great difference between going *against* the Constitution's provisions and "merely" adding to it. The fact is that adding to it is one way of going against it by changing it.

27. How much the Court-packing plan can be credited for the Court's switch, however, is a matter of some dispute. See Frankfurter, "Mr. Justice Roberts," *University of Pennsylvania Law Review* 104 (1955): 313, for a convincing argument that Roberts's due process views antedated the Court-packing plan. And in the commerce clause area, the author of *National Labor Relations Board* v. *Jones-Laughlin* was Chief Justice Hughes, who had written a broad commerce clause opinion many years earlier (1914) in *The Shreveport Case.* Nonetheless, when one considers the *magnitude* of the Court switch—its virtual abdication of review in economic regulation cases—then the image of the Court bowing before the storm is more convincing.

28. For a strongly contrary argument, in fact, see Justice Sutherland's dissents in *Home Building and Loan* v. *Blaisdell*, 290 U.S. 398 (1934); and *West Coast Hotel* v. *Parrish*, 300 U.S. 379 (1937).

29. For an argument to this effect, see Jacobsohn, *Pragmatism, Statesmanship, and the Supreme Court* (Ithaca, N.Y.: Cornell University Press, 1977), chapt. 2.

30. Wilson, *Constitutional Government in the United States* (New York: Columbia University Press, 1908).

31. Holmes, *The Common Law* (Boston: Little, Brown, 1881).

32. For a developed expression of these views, see Cardozo, *The Nature of the Judicial Process*.

33. *Kovacs* v. *Cooper*, 336 U.S. 77, 95 (1949).

34. *Brown* v. *Board of Education*, 347 U.S. 492.

35. On the equity power of federal courts, see McDowell, *Equity and the Constitution: The Supreme Court, Equitable Relief, and Public Policy* (Chicago: University of Chicago Press, 1982), especially chapts. 6 and 7.

36. Another phrase that might have been employed more, but for its narrow reading in The Slaughterhouse Cases, 16 Wallace 36 (1873), is the privileges and immunities clause.

37. I am describing modern judicial review as it is understood by some contemporary constitutional commentators and defenders of Court activism. The Supreme Court is more reticent about acknowledging the legislative character of its power, although occasionally a justice will make an observation about it. Some justices, however, would deny it; Justice Hugo Black is the outstanding example. Black claimed to interpret the Constitution according to principles that appear to be much more traditional than modern. A close look at his jurisprudence, however, suggests that this is not the case, for reasons I discuss in a review of Gerald Dunne's biography of Black in *The American Spectator* 10 (11) (October, 1977).

Other constitutional commentators today would strongly deny that it is fair to characterize the shift in judicial review as one from "interpretation" to "legislation." The key difference between us would be over the latitude that may fairly be given the term *interpretation*. Implicit in my approach is a denial that specifying such generalities as liberty, equality, and human dignity could fairly be called interpretation. For a contrary view, see Dworkin, *Taking Rights Seriously* (Cambridge: Harvard University Press, 1977), especially chapts. 4 and 5, "Hard Cases" and "Constitutional Cases" and *Law's Empire* (Cambridge: Harvard University Press, 1986).

38. Bickel, *The Least Dangerous Branch*, chapt.1.
39. The changes in the case and controversy requirement are not merely the result of judicial assertion. Some of the expansion has occurred with the active support of Congress. For example, the power of federal courts to issue "declaratory judgments"—rulings prior to actual attempts by government to deprive someone of rights they claim—rests on congressional legislation.
40. This is not to say that people were insensitive to the broad implications of judicial review earlier. Obviously, one of the most salient features of judicial review is that it implies a judicial power that reaches far beyond the individual case. But the traditional era was far more sensitive to the origins of judicial review and especially to the fact that it was "derivative" from a more fundamental power. Thus, justices like Chief Justice Marshall could accept with perfect equanimity the possibility that some constitutional issues were beyond the purview of the judiciary, because they could not reach it in the form of a case. Marshall said the Constitution "does not extend the judicial power to every violation of the constitution which may possibly take place, but to 'a case in law or equity,' in which a right, under such law, is asserted in a court of justice. If the question cannot be brought into a court, then there is no case in law or equity, and no jurisdiction is given." (*Cohens* v. *Virginia,* 6 Wheaton 264, 405 [1819])
41. On standing, see Abraham, *The Judicial Process*, 5th ed. (New York: Oxford University Press, 1986), pp. 370–375; and also Kristol, "The American Judicial Power and the American Regime," Ph.D. diss., Harvard University, 1979.
42. Ely, *Democracy and Distrust: A Theory of Judicial Review* (Cambridge: Harvard University Press, 1980), p. 14.
43. 304 U.S. 152 (1938).
44. 369 U.S. 186 (1962).
45. *Powell* v. *McCormack*, 395 U.S. 486 (1969)
46. *Marbury* v. *Madison,* 1 Cranch 177
47. For a fascinating revisionist discussion of *Marbury* as an argument for a very narrow form of judicial review and of the subsequent history of the use of *Marbury*, see Clinton, *Marbury* v. *Madison and Judicial Review* (Lawrence: University Press of Kansas, 1989).
48. 358 U.S. 1 (1958).
49. Cited in Henry Abraham, *The Judicial Process*, p. 341 n. 38.

Chapter One

1. 252 U.S. 416, 433 (1920).
2. 290 U.S. 398, 442-43 (1934).
3. Wilson, *Congressional Government* (Gloucester, Mass.: Peter Smith, 1973), p. 203.
4. Wilson, *Constitutional Government in the United States* (New York: Columbia University Press, 1908), p. 168.
5. Wilson, *Congressional Government*, pp. 54–55.
6. On the "incorporation" of the Bill of Rights' guarantees of criminal defendants' rights into the Fourteenth Amendment due process clause, see *Duncan* v. *Louisiana*, 391 U.S. 145 (1968); and Berger, *Government by Judiciary: The Transformation of the Fourteenth Amendment*. (Cambridge: Harvard University Press, 1977), chapt. 8.
7. Civil Rights Cases, 109 U.S. 3 (1883); *Jones* v. *Alfred H. Mayer Co.*, 392 U.S. 409, 449 (1968) (Justice Harlan dissenting).
8. *Goesaert* v. *Cleary*, 335 U.S. 464 (1948); *Craig* v. *Boren*, 429 U.S. 190, 217 (1976) (Justice Rehnquist dissenting).
9. *Douglas* v. *California*, 372 U.S. 353, 360 (1963) (Justice Harlan dissenting); *James* v. *Valtierra*, 402 U.S. 137 (1971).
10. *Roe* v. *Wade*, 410 U.S. 113, 221 (1973) (Justice White dissenting).
11. On the original scope of freedom of speech, see Levy, *Legacy of Suppression* (New York: Harper & Row, 1963). On religion, see Cord, *Separation of Church and State* (New York: Lambeth Press, 1982); and Bradley, *Church–State Relationships in America* (New York: Greenwood Press, 1987).
12. See, for example, *Wickard* v. *Filburn*, 317 U.S. 111 (1942).
13. Levy, *Legacy of Suppression*.
14. On Madison's views and their limited impact on the First Amendment, see Michael Malbin, *Religion and Politics: The Intentions of the Authors of the First Amendment* (Washington, D.C.: American Enterprise Institute, 1978).
15. A good discussion of the Founders' views on slavery can be found in Diamond, *The Democratic Republic*, 2d ed. (Chicago: Rand McNally, 1970).
16. On the limits of public opinion, see Berger *Government By Judiciary*, chapt. 1. Berger is generally accurate, if a bit stark, in his description.

17. Wilson, *Congressional Government*, p. 163. Another classic attack on the amending process can be found in J. Allen Smith, *The Spirit of American Government* (New York: Macmillan, 1911).
18. Wilson, *Congressional Government*, pp. 55, 164.
19. See Ackerman, "Discovering the Constitution," *Yale Law Journal* 93 (1984): 1013, 1052–1057.
20. Cf. Martin Diamond, *The Founding of the Democratic Republic* (Itasca, Ill.: F.E. Peacock, 1981), chapt. 2.
21. For positivist-oriented opposition to judicial activism, see Berger, *Government by Judiciary*, chapt. 14; and Lino A. Graglia, "Was the Constitution a Good Idea?," *National Review*, July 13, 1984. Chief Justice Rehnquist and Judge Robert Bork have been characterized as positivist opponents of judicial activism, and their vocabulary (especially that of constitutional "values") often suggests this. I am not so sure that they are thoroughly positivists. For a critique of Berger on this point, see Gary Jacobsohn, "Hamilton, Positivism, and the Constitution: Judicial Discretion Reconsidered," *Polity* (Fall, 1981) 14 (1), pp. 70–88.
22. See, for example, Ackerman, "Discovering the Constitution."
23. *National League of Cities* v. *Usery*, 426 U.S. 833 (1976), it could be argued, was an attempt to put some limits on the modern commerce power. But it did so in a rather narrow area—the prerogative of states to regulate their own employees—and more important, was overruled after only a few years, in *Garcia* v. *San Antonio*, 469 U.S. 528 (1985). As things stand now, the only federal constitutional limits on the commerce power are liberty and equality concerns arising from other constitutional prohibitions, such as freedom of speech.
24. Another form of change would be the Court's adoption of new "constitutional" principles. But this change resolves itself into the question of whether the judiciary is the appropriate amender. This question involves arguments that will be taken up in subsequent chapters.
25. See, for example, Felix Morley, *Freedom and Federalism* (Chicago: Regnery, 1959).
26. The classic exposition of this power is *McCulloch* v. *Maryland*, 4 Wheaton 316 (1819), especially at 415.
27. Diamond, *The Democratic Republic*, p. 119.
28. Note, for example, Berger's discussion in chapter 17 of *Government by Judiciary*.

Chapter Two

1. Bickel, *The Least Dangerous Branch* (Indianapolis: Bobbs-Merrill, 1962); Ely, *Democracy and Distrust: A Theory of Judicial Review* (Cambridge: Harvard University Press, 1980); Choper, *Judicial Review and the National Political Process: A Functional Reconsideration of the Role of the Supreme Court* (Chicago: University of Chicago Press, 1980).
2. A particularly fine discussion of the relative democratic credentials of the different branches can be found in Choper, *Judicial Review*, chapt. 1.
3. For an approach of this kind, see Eidelberg, *The Philosophy of the American Constitution* (New York: Free Press, 1968), chapt. 10.
4. *Federalist* No. 78, pp. 395–396, makes this "democratic defense" of judicial review.
5. *Federalist*, No. 51, p. 264.
6. *Federalist*, No. 10, pp. 46–49.
7. Note that the classic exposition of separation of powers, in *Federalist*, No. 51, pp. 261–265, focuses primarily on the relation between Congress and the legislature. Particularly striking is the absence of any reference to judicial review in that number.
8. Levy, *Legacy of Suppression* (Cambridge: Harvard University Press, 1960); Berns, *The First Amendment and the Future of American Democracy* (New York: Basic Books, 1976); Berger, *Government by Judiciary: The Transformation of the Fourteenth Amendment* (Cambridge: Harvard University Press, 1977).
9. McKeon, *The Basic Works of Aristotle* (New York: Random House, 1941), pp. 1265–1266.
10. When I say that the Declaration seems to confirm Aristotle, I mean that it exemplifies the democratic emphasis on liberty, not that it agrees with him. Aristotle would argue that the purpose of government is not merely the protection of rights, but the achievement of the common good, including the moral and intellectual virtue of the citizenry. The Declaration's narrower view of the purpose of government reflects its elevation of liberty to the chief goal, which Aristotle would consider defective but—because the United States is a democratic republic—understandable.

    At the same time, the original American regime did include certain "nonliberal" elements, which focused more on duties than rights, as, for example, the favorable status of religion and traditional family duties in state law. Aristotle would have considered these to be healthy balancing elements in the regime, perhaps making it more like what he called a "polity" than a pure democracy.

11. A classic defense of modern judicial review based on its furthering of democratic ends is Rostow, "The Democratic Character of Judicial Review," *Harvard Law Review* 66 (1952): 193.

12. 304 U.S. 144, 152 n.4 (1938).

13. Of the three prongs to the *Carolene Products* rationale, this first is closest to a traditional approach, as long as Stone's language is taken strictly; that is, he says that there may be "narrower scope for operation of the presumption of constitutionality" in these cases. Interpreted literally, that means that there still is such a presumption. Interestingly, according to Louis Lusky, a clerk for Justice Stone at the time, this part of the *Carolene Products* footnote was not from Stone, but from Chief Justice Charles Hughes, a somewhat less "modern" justice. Cf. Lusky, *By What Right? A Commentary on the Supreme Court's Power to Revise the Constitution* (Charlottesville, Va.: The Michie Co., 1976), p. 110. In fact, though, this aspect of the *Carolene Products* footnote is invoked almost exclusively for certain constitutional rights (e.g., First Amendment rights) and not others (e.g., the contract clause), and this lack of evenhandedness suggests a certain result orientation rather than a traditional approach to interpretation.

14. *Federalist*, No. 51, p. 264

15. On changes during Lincoln's and Johnson's presidencies, see Abraham, *Justices and Presidents* (New York: Oxford University Press, 1974).

16. On the possibility of noncompliance, see Baum, *The Supreme Court* (Washington, D.C.: Congressional Quarterly, 1981), pp. 179–198.

17. Choper, *Judicial Review*, p. 49, n. 133.

18. See Thomas Jefferson's letter to James Madison, September 6, 1789, in *The Works of Thomas Jefferson*, ed. Washington (Philadelphia: Lippincott, 1869) 3: 102.

19. For example, in a series of polls taken in 1966, 1973, 1974, 1976, 1977, 1978, and 1979, the ABC News–Harris Survey found that "high confidence" was placed in the Supreme Court, more so than in either Congress or the executive. See ABC News–Harris Survey vol. 1, no. 27 (March 5, 1979).

20. 347 U.S. 483(1954).

21. 369 U.S. 186 (1962).

22. Choper, *Judicial Review*, p. 133.

23. Tocqueville, *Democracy in America*, vol. II (New York: Random House, Vintage, 1945), Book II, chapt. 1, argues that "freedom has appeared in the world at different times and under various forms; it has not been exclusively bound to any social condition, and it is not confined to democracies" (p. 100).

24. 1 Cranch 137 (1803).

25. Ely, for example, contends that the privileges and immunities clause, the equal protection clause, and the Ninth Amendment are open-ended provisions that invite judicial enforcement of rights not listed in the document itself. Cf. *Democracy and Distrust*, chapt. 2.

26. *Federalist,* No. 10, p. 90.

27. I do not mean to imply that there is no clear constitutional guidance in these examples. Although there is no guidance with respect to issues such as abortion, there is at least some guidance with respect to criminal defendants' rights, for example.

28. On the limits of the formal checks, see Ely, *Democracy and Distrust*, pp. 46–47.

29. *Federalist,* No. 65, p. 331.

30. *Federalist,* No. 49, p. 256. See also McDowell, "On Meddling with the Constitution," *Journal of Contemporary Studies* V, no. 4 (Fall 1982).

31. 4 Wheaton 316, 407 (1819).

32. For an able defense of the constitutionality of using the power over jurisdiction to limit the Court, see Rossum, "Congress, the Constitution, and the Appellate Jurisdiction of the Supreme Court: The Letter and the Spirit of the Exceptions Clause," *William and Mary Law Review* 12 (April 1983).

33. I know of no evidence to suggest that the framers intended these congressional powers to be used as checks on the Court, rather than for technical or administrative purposes.

34. Why does obscenity have to have the same legal definition in Alabama and in New York, for example? Apart from the desirability of a "floor" and a "ceiling" on what could be prohibited, can't reasonable people disagree over exactly where the line should be drawn? And if so, why should that indeterminacy automatically mandate the imposition of a more libertarian approach?

35. Scigliano, *The Supreme Court and the Presidency* (New York: Free Press, 1971), p. 157.

36. School desegregation in the South, for example, advanced very slowly until 1964, when the passage of the Civil Rights Act and its provision

for cutting off federal funds speeded the process greatly. Cf. Lusky, *By What Right?* p. 218.

37. The classic case—the historical accuracy of which is uncertain—was Andrew Jackson's tart remark, "Well, John Marshall has made his decision, now let him enforce it," in regard to *Worcester* v. *Georgia,* 6 Peters 515 (1832); see Scigliano, *The Supreme Court and the Presidency,* p. 36.

38. Ibid, p. 60.

39. I realize that this overstates the case somewhat. Not everything that gets through Congress has broad popular support. With respect to matters that the popular majority *knows* and *cares* about, however, this is generally accurate.

40. For matters that concern the people, the Court would need the support of a significant minority. But this would hardly reconcile one to the antimajoritarian character of this action. How many Americans would have been reconciled to a Goldwater presidency in 1964 simply because he represented a significant minority?

41. James Madison gave testimony to the weight of precedent when he signed the second bank bill, although his abstract opinion on the constitutional question had not changed since the time he led congressional opposition to it on constitutional grounds. See Hunt, ed., *The Writings of James Madison,* vol. IX (New York: Putnam's Sons, 1900–1910), pp. 442–443 (letter to C. E. Haynes February 25, 1831). Justice John Paul Stevens is a modern example of a justice who adheres to a precedent that he is convinced was wrongly decided in *Runyon* v. *McCrary,* 427 U.S. 160, 189 (1976). He argued that *Jones* v. *Mayer,* 392 U.S. 409 (1968) was incorrect in asserting that Section 1 of the Civil Rights Act of 1866 prohibited private racial discrimination but contended that it ought not to be overruled because it accords with the prevailing sense of justice today.

42. As President Lincoln said, in regard to asking a potential appointee how he would vote in a case: "if we should, and he should answer us, we should despise him for it," cited in Scigliano, *The Supreme Court and the President* p. 120, from Warren, *The Supreme Court in U.S. History,* Vol. II, (Boston: Little, Brown, 1922) p. 401.

43. Nominees rarely answer in more than the vaguest generalities during Senate hearings. If fidelity to the Constitution is a criterion for a good Supreme Court justice, then why should a senator be precluded from knowing the nominee's general understanding of important constitutional provisions?

44. For the pro-business orientation of the legal profession at the end of the nineteenth century, see Twiss, *Lawyers and the Constitution* (Princeton: Princeton University Press, 1942); and Paul, *Conservative Crisis and the Rule of Law* (New York: Harper Torchbooks, 1969).

45. Cf. Choper, *Judicial Review*, pp. 16–24.

46. Cf. Ely, *Democracy and Distrust*, p. 70; and Black, *The People and the Court* (New York: Macmillan, 1960). For a particular area, see Muir, *Law and Attitude Change: Prayer in the Public Schools* (Chicago: University of Chicago Press, 1973).

47. Choper, *Judicial Review*, pp. 92–94.

48. Cf. Lusky, *By What Right?* p. 343.

49. Martin Shapiro points out that *Miller* v. *California*, 413 U.S. 5 (1973), was only a "slight rollback" of Warren Court policies. "The Supreme Court: From Warren to Burger," in *The New American Political System*, ed. King (Washington, D.C.: American Enterprise Institute, 1978), p. 204.

50. On the connection between law, court decisions, the tone of society, and community moral standards, see Clor, *Obscenity and Public Morality* (Chicago: University of Chicago Press, 1968).

51. James Madison noted the general principle in *Federalist*, No. 49, p. 256: ". . . the strength of opinion in each individual, and its practical influence on his conduct, depend much on the number which he supposes to have entertained the same opinion. The reason of man, like man himself, is timid and cautious when left alone, and acquires firmness and confidence in proportion to the number with which it is associated."

52. That is why Abraham Lincoln believed that the United States could not long endure as half-slave and half-free, even if the views of Democratic moderates like Stephen Douglas prevailed. Douglas's position of popular sovereignty (let the people of the territories decide for themselves on slavery; he didn't care how they decided, he said) implied a refusal of the nation to maintain its original commitment to extinguish slavery in the long run; and if the nation became morally neutral on the issue of slavery, the nation's traditional principles—those of the Declaration of Independence, contrary to slavery—would be eroded over time. See especially Lincoln's "House Divided" speech in Springfield, accepting the Republican nomination for Illinois senator, June 16, 1858, *The Political Thought of Abraham Lincoln*, ed. Current (Indianapolis: Bobbs-Merrill, 1967) pp. 94–103.

53. Cf. Bruce-Biggs, *The New Class* (New Brunswick, N.J.: Transaction Books, 1979), p. 202; see also Ladd's article in the same book "Pursuing

the New Class: Social Theory and Survey Data," especially pp. 106–108, and Bell's "A Muddled Concept," especially pp. 186–187.

54. For example, while the anti-abortion movement in the United States, had begun before *Roe* v. *Wade* in 1973, it really became a major factor in American political and social life only after the Court's pro-abortion decision. See Luker, *Abortion and the Politics of Motherhood* (Berkeley: University of California Press, 1984).

55. Cf. Wilson, *Political Organization* (New York: Basic Books, 1973).

56. This argument is less "democratic" than previous ones, because it does not assume the independent citizen of democratic theory, whose thought and action are a result simply of free choice. If attitudes of future citizens are "shaped" by a Court's decision, one might respond to the argument, those attitudes are free and uncoerced nonetheless and their prevailing would not offend the democratic principle. What *does* offend it, however, is that present majorities are subordinated to the minority power represented by the judiciary in the conflict over who will make the laws that help form the attitudes of future citizens.

57. *Los Angeles Times* poll, in *Public Opinion* (August/September 1982) p. 25.

58. Of course, *Roe* v. *Wade* went far beyond this, since abortions in the second trimester could be limited only in the interest of maternal health, and were permissible in the last trimester if the life and the health (physical and mental) of the mother were threatened. This question, however, focuses only on the part of pregnancy when abortion is unambiguously an absolute right.

59. Cardozo, *The Nature of the Judicial Process* (New Haven: Yale University Press, 1921), p. 10. Cardozo specifically notes that this refers not just to common law but to statutory and constitutional interpretation as well (p. 14).

60. A good recent example was the reaction among legal commentators to Berger, *Government by Judiciary*. See, for example, *Hastings Constitutional Law Quarterly* 6, no. 2 (Winter, 1979).

61. 384 U.S. 436 (1966).

62. Bickel, *The Least Dangerous Branch*, p. 74; *United States* v. *Nixon*, 418 U.S. 683 (1974) at 703.

63. Cf. the Introduction. I realize that even what may honestly be called "interpretation" of the Constitution has its difficulties. My point here is not that interpretation is always easy or obvious—that is clearly not so. It is that modern constitutional interpretation *necessarily* and admittedly involves a great deal of judicial "will," or judicial policy-making,

because it is based on allegedly open-ended generalities. Although this is taken for granted in law schools, defenders of judicial activism (and above all the Court itself) typically do not take this view to the American people.

64. To use a rough analogy: The acquittal of Federalist Justice Samuel Chase on impeachment charges in 1805 did not reflect the tacit consent of the Republican Senate to his partisan speech on the bench (the basis for the impeachment), but rather their fear that giving Chase his just desserts would permanently damage the judiciary.

65. Berger, *Government by Judiciary*, chapt. 7.

66. For example, clearly there have been essential changes in the nature of American federalism, in that states no longer have ultimate policy-making power in virtually any area, except by the sufferance of the national government. It may be arguable that the American people have tacitly consented to this change. At the same time, one wonders whether the nation might have benefited from genuine national deliberation, through the amendment process, about the form and extent of such a change, and whether the absence of such deliberation may not have resulted in a somewhat more radical shift than would have been intended upon deliberation. For further discussion, see Wolfe, "The Contemporary Supreme Court and Federalism," in *Federalism and the Constitution: A Symposium on Garcia* (Washington, D.C.: Advisory Commission on Intergovernmental Relations, 1987).

67. See a summary and criticism of such views in Lawrence, "Procedural Norms and Tolerance: A Reassessment," *American Political Science Review* 70, no. 1 (March 1976): pp. 80–100.

Chapter Three

1. Justice Robert Jackson makes this argument in *The Supreme Court in the American System of Government* (Cambridge: Harvard University Press, 1958), p. 11–12.

2. McCloskey, *The American Supreme Court* (Chicago: University of Chicago Press, 1960),p. 223–224.

3. For discussion of the influence of legal periodicals, see Abraham, *The Judicial Process*, 5th ed. (New York: Oxford University Press, 1980), pp. 243–245; on the character of the legal profession, see Tocqueville, *Democracy in America*, vol. I (New York: Random House, Vintage, 1945), chapt. 16, pp. 282–290.

4. For an excellent discussion of this issue see Choper, *Judicial Review and the National Political Process: A Functional Reconsideration of the Role of the Supreme Court* (Chicago: University of Chicago Press, 1980), pp. 12–24 (on Congress) and pp. 46–47 (on the president).

5. 372 U.S. 335 (1963).

6. *Gideon* v. *Wainwright*, for example, overturned the Court's previous holding (a sort of "due-process common law" holding) in *Betts* v. *Brady*, which had upheld state practices based partly on statute and partly on common law.

7. For example, *Jenkins* v. *Georgia*, 418 U.S. 153 (1974) overturned the conviction of a theater for showing the movie *Carnal Knowledge*.

8. For example, *Cantwell* v. *Connecticut*, 310 U.S. 296 (1940), *Lovell* v. *Griffin*, 303 U.S. 444 (1938).

9. *Griswold* v. *Connecticut*, 381 U.S. 479 (1965).

10. Choper's defense of judicial activism with regard to civil liberties rests heavily on the argument of "good results." *Judicial Review*, pp. 79–122.

11. Ibid., p. 92.

12. For example, *Barenblatt* v. *United States*, 360 U.S. 109 (1959).

13. For example, *Watkins* v. *United States*, 354 U.S. 178 (1957); and *Yates* v. *United States*, 354 U.S. 298 (1957). See Wilson, *American Government*, 2nd ed. (Lexington, Mass.: D.C. Heath, 1983), p. 497.

14. On these attacks, see Murphy, *Congress and the Court* (Chicago: University of Chicago Press, 1962); and Pritchett, *Congress versus the Supreme Court* (Minneapolis: University of Minnesota Press, 1961).

15. Moreover, the fact that the Court was moderate in the protection of such rights–such as in refusing to uphold draft-card burning as a free speech right, *United States* v. *O'Brien*, 391 U.S. 367 (1968), and in rejecting a demand for selective conscientious objection as a religious right, *Gillette* v. *United States*, 401 U.S. 437 (1971)—while disappointing to some scholars, is considered by others to demonstrate that the power is used in a limited and responsible way, with a reasonable recognition of competing social values.

16. See, for example, Manwaring, *Render unto Caesar: The Flag Salute Controversy* (Chicago: University of Chicago Press, 1962); *Sherbert* v. *Verner*, 374 U.S. 398 (1963).

17. For a typical attack on malapportionment, see Dixon, *Democratic Representation* (New York: Oxford University Press, 1968).

18. *Baker* v. *Carr*, 369 U.S. 186, 270 (1962).

19. Choper, *Judicial Review*, p. 102.

20. Cf. *Gideon* v. *Wainwright*, 372 U.S. 335 (1963).

21. At the time of *Gideon*, five states did not automatically provide counsel to indigents in noncapital felony cases. Choper, *Judicial Review*, p. 97.
22. *Mapp* v. *Ohio*, 367 U.S. 643 (1961).
23. *Miranda* v. *Arizona*, 384 U.S. 436 (1966).
24. *Furman* v. *Georgia*, 408 U.S. 238 (1972); *Gregg* v. *Georgia*, 428 U.S. 153 (1976); *Woodson* v. *North Carolina*, 428 U.S. 280 (1976); *Coker* v. *Georgia*, 433 U.S. 584 (1977); and *Lockett* v. *Ohio*, 438 U.S. 586 (1978).
25. *Griswold* v. *Connecticut*, 381 U.S. 479 (1965); *Roe* v. *Wade*, 410 U.S. 113 (1973).
26. Some recent scholarship has focused on the question of "comparative institutional capacity" in its evaluation of judicial activity. See, for example, Horowitz, *The Courts and Social Policy* (Washington, D.C.: Brookings, 1977); and Cavanaugh and Sarat, "Thinking About Courts: Toward and Beyond a Jurisprudence of Judicial Competence," *Law and Society Review* 14 (1979–1980): 371.
27. On the eminence of appointees to the Supreme Court, see Scigliano, *The Supreme Court and the Presidency* (New York: Free Press, 1971), pp. 107–108.
28. Cf. Choper, *Judicial Review*, pp. 68–69.
29. Bickel, *The Least Dangerous Branch* (Indianapolis: Bobbs-Merrill, 1962), pp. 25–26.
30. Abraham, *The Judicial Process*, p. 362.
31. McCloskey, *The American Supreme Court*, pp. 174–178.
32. Cf. Pritchett, *Congress versus the Supreme Court*.
33. This is one of the central themes of McCloskey, *The American Supreme Court*, a history of the Court that ends, however, in the 1950s. See also Dahl, "The Supreme Court's Role in National Policy-Making," *Journal of Public Law* 6 (1957): 279.
34. For example, James Q. Wilson has described four kinds of legislation; the categories are produced by the possible combinations of two factors, costs and benefits. Two of the four categories involve laws that do not have broad public support: (1) interest group politics, where costs and benefits are concentrated on particular groups, and (2) client politics, where benefits are concentrated but the costs are very diffused and therefore little noticed. *American Government*, 3d ed. (Lexington, Mass.: D.C. Heath, 1986) pp. 428–434.

The law referred to in the text (the limitation to twenty years of a prohibition on using buildings built with federal funds for religious purposes) was struck down in *Tilton* v. *Richardson*, 403 U.S. 672 (1971).

35. Cf. Choper, *Judicial Review*, p. 25.

36. Cf. Lusky, *By What Right?* (Charlottesville, Va.: The Michie Co., 1975), p. 292.

37. 392 U.S. 83 (1968).

38. Lusky, p. 177.

39. 412 U.S. 669,688 (1973).

40. See, for example, *Schlesinger* v. *Reservists*, 418 U.S. 208 (1974); *United States* v. *Richardson*, 418 U.S. 166 (1974); and *Warth* v. *Seldin*, 422 U.S. 490 (1975).

41. Unless one takes seriously Justice William D. Douglas's invocation in *Griswold* v. *Connecticut*, 381 U.S. 479 (1965), of opinions written by Justice James C. McReynolds, perhaps the most reactionary twentieth-century Supreme Court justice, in *Pierce* v. *Society of Sisters*, 268 U.S. 510 (1925); and *Meyer* v. *Nebraska*, 262 U.S. 390 (1923)!

42. Cf. Twiss, *Lawyers and the Constitution* (Princeton: Princeton University Press, 1942).

43. This latter sense could be regarded as a "weaker" one, since representatives do not always reflect popular opinion exactly. But insofar as deliberation by representatives is considered a means of elevating and refining public opinion, as *Federalist*, No. 10 argues (pp. 46–47), *while still being subject to its control at elections*, this sense may, of course, be a stronger sense in principle. Cf. Bessette, "Deliberative Democracy: The Majority Principle in Republican Government," in *How Democratic is the Constitution?* ed. Goldwin and Schambra (Washington, D.C.: American Enterprise Institute, 1980).

44. For a critique of the "good results" argument, see Gangi, "Judicial Expansionism: An Evaluation of the Ongoing Debate," *Ohio Northern Law Review* 8 (1981): 57ff.

45. Court cases by themselves initially had limited impact on the actual number of southern children in integrated schools.

46. *Swann* v. *Charlotte-Mecklenberg*, 402 U.S. 1 (1971); *Keyes* v. *Denver School District*, 413 U.S. 921 (1973). See Graglia, *Disaster by Decree: The Supreme Court Decision on Race and the Schools* (Ithaca, N.Y.: Cornell University Press, 1976), chaps. 7–10. For a defense of busing, see Orfield, *Must We Bus? Segregated Schools and National Policy* (Washington, D.C.: Brookings, 1978).

47. On blacks and busing, see *Newsweek* poll, March 9, 1981, p. 29, and Lichter, "Who Speaks for Black America," *Public Opinion*, August/September 1985, p. 43.

48. Graglia, *Disaster by Decree*, chapt. 11.
49. See, for example, Rossum, *Reverse Discrimination* (New York: Marcel Dekker, 1980).
50. Cf. Lusky, *By What Right?* pp. 343, 362–363.
51. See, for example, Downs, *The New Politics of Pornography* (Chicago: University of Chicago Press, 1989).
52. See Justice William H. Rehnquist's dissent in *Thomas* v. *Review Board*, 450 U.S. 707 (1981).
53. See, for example, Bradley, "Dogmatomachy—A Privatization Theory of the Religion Clause Cases," *St. Louis Law Journal* 30 (1986): 275.
54. See *WMCA* v. *Lomenzo*, 377 U.S. 633 (1964); and *Lucas* v. *Colorado*, 377 U.S. 713 (1964); especially Justice Potter Stewart's dissent at p. 744. For a broader attack on the Court's entire reapportionment undertaking, see Justice John Harlan's dissent at p. 589, and, Elliott, *The Rise of Guardian Democracy* (Cambridge: Harvard University Press, 1974).
55. For a critical analysis of the effect of many Court decisions in this area, see Fleming, *The Price of Perfect Justice* (New York: Basic Books, 1974), especially parts I and II.
56. Rice, *Beyond Abortion* (Chicago: Franciscan Herald Press, 1979)
57. Interestingly, Choper, in his review of results of Court decisions in *Judicial Review*, treats these cases rather gingerly, noting some grounds for defense and one critic's comments.
58. Gangi, "Judicial Expansionism," pp. 65–67.
59. Epstein, *Takings: Private Property and the Power of Eminent Domain* (Cambridge: Harvard University Press, 1985).
60. Mott, *Due Process of Law* (Indianapolis: Bobbs-Merrill, 1926).
61. This seems to be the tone of Benjamin Cardozo's remarks in *The Nature of the Judicial Process* (New Haven: Yale University Press, 1925), pp. 76–81.
62. Ely, *Democracy and Distrust*, pp. 69–70.
63. See, for example, Bruce-Biggs, *The New Class?* (New Brunswick N.J.: Transaction Books, 1979), especially Glazer's article "Lawyers and the New Class."
64. Above, n. 42.
65. If freedom from political pressure leads to greater impartiality and thereby justifies a greater share of political power, then kings and aristocrats have had a good case for political power. In fact, one of the arguments sometimes used for hereditary kingship was analogous. When discussing foreign affairs, the framers of the Constitution noted that one of the real problems in democracies had been that public officials were subject to bribery, since their power could end and they

might be tempted to keep an eye on their personal future. Kings, being hereditary and therefore substantially independent of such concerns, were relatively immune to such inducements.

Nor could one argue that judges are subject to external limitations, whereas hereditary kings and nobles were not. In fact, the idea of "absolute kingship" is for the most part a historical myth. There was almost always a "balance of power" among a variety of political actors in monarchies, especially aristocrats, clergy, and guilds. Moreover, custom was a more powerful force limiting political action in monarchies than it is in democracies. It is an open question whether past hereditary monarchs or contemporary Supreme Court justices have had more practical power to bring about, through law, profound changes in the life of a nation, without the support of a majority of its citizens.

66. Thomas Hobbes, for example, considered the greatest source of political evils to be various opinions about good and evil, and religious opinions were among the chief sources of such problems. And if Hobbes considered religious opinions to be the self-interested opinions of ecclesiastics who pursued political power, it would be easy enough to draw an analogy between that analysis and criticism of modern judges.

67. Cf. Shapiro, "The Supreme Court: From Warren to Burger," in *The New American Political System*, ed. King (Washington: American Enterprise Institute, 1978), p. 199. On the Court's workload, see Lusky, *By What Right?* pp. 351–355.

68. To the extent that these are minimized as "rationalizations" compiled by the legislative staff on the basis of information provided by self-interested parties, one might suggest that opinions written in great part by law clerks employing arguments from counsel to rationalize judicial decisions may not be all that different.

69. Legislators may have a personal interest in finding busing an inadequate tool, since it is very unpopular with their constituents. This is an example of the argument that judges are more detached than legislators, and so they can be more impartial or detached. It is not clear, on the other hand, that judges approach the issue any differently. Ideologically liberal justices are likely to be just as one-sided in their evaluation of the utility of busing as legislators on the other side.

On judicial capacity to deal with social science evidence, see also Horowitz, *The Courts and Social Policy*, pp. 25, 31, 45–51, 274–84.

70. Ibid., pp. 34–35, 255–257.

71. Ibid., p. 36.

72. Cf. Diamond, Fisk, and Garfinkel, *The Democratic Republic* (Chicago: Rand McNally, 1966), chapt. 6.
73. For example, how might a good many federal judges rule on the issue of polygamy (or polyandry) if it came to them today as a fresh issue (i.e., apart from firm precedent upholding laws prohibiting it)? Given the "privacy" issue involved, and possible religious considerations in some cases, such laws would require a compelling state interest and least restrictive means. The social interest in monogamy is important, but it is not that immediate or tangible. The social interest would consist especially in avoiding greater occasions for disputes within the family and avoiding the discrimination and inequality likely to afflict some spouses. If it were to be balanced against religious claims of a typical Mormon polygamous unit (as in the 1878 case *Reynolds* v. *United States*, 98 U.S. 145), where (like the Amish in *Wisconsin* v. *Yoder*, 406 U.S. 205 [1972]) there would be a record of decent, law-abiding, orderly habits, the Mormons might win today, given modern free exercise law (at least before *Employment Division* v. *Smith*, 108 L.Ed 2d 876 [1990]) and the intangibility of the public interest in monogamy. (And if a Mormon might win today, polygamy based on secular beliefs would claim equal rights relative to religiously based polygamy.) Libertarians might hail such a decision, but traditionalists would ask whether the American family needs to be weakened still further, and egalitarians might well worry about its effects as well, for different reasons (such as sexual equality).
74. For a similar line of reasoning, see Tocqueville's remarks on why Americans value equality even more than liberty, in *Democracy in America*, vol. II, book II, chapt. 1.
75. See Bond, *The Art of Judging* (New Brunswick, N.J.: Transaction Books, 1987), chapt. 7.
76. Hand, *The Bill of Rights* (Cambridge: Harvard University Press, 1958), p. 73.
77. *Federalist* No. 81, p. 411.
78. No doubt the framers would have provided a much more readily usable check on the judiciary if they had decided to give the courts as much power as they now have. What *kind* of check they would have provided is a matter of speculation. Some possibilities include requiring an extraordinary majority to strike down a law, allowing an extraordinary congressional majority to override the judicial "veto," providing judges with a fairly long limited term of office without reeligibility. But the framers did not think along these lines because they did not consider

judges' "public law" activities, such as judicial review, their main function. Judicial review was understood to be a rare act, an occasionally necessary *incident* of the judiciary's primarily *private law* function of deciding cases. On this point, see Kristol, *The American Judicial Power and the American Regime* (Ph.D. diss., Harvard University, 1979); and Snowiss, "From Fundamental Law to the Supreme Law of the Land: A Reinterpretation of the Origin of Judicial Review in the United States" (paper delivered at the 1981 American Political Science Association annual meeting, New York, Sept. 3–6, 1981.)

79. Cf. Goebel, *History of the Supreme Court of the United States: Antecedents and Beginnings to 1801* (New York: Macmillan, 1971), p. 240. The earliest attempted use of the power for "checking" purposes—the attempts to deprive the Court of jurisdiction over appeals from the highest state courts by repealing Section 25 of the Judiciary Act of 1789—were concerned with "structural" questions of federalism rather than more specific substantive constitutional questions, although they were spurred on by dissatisfaction with Marshall Court decisions.

80. See Rossum, "Congress, the Constitution, and the Appellate Jurisdiction of the Supreme Court: The Letter and the Spirit of the Exceptions Clause," 24 *William and Mary Law Review* 385 (April, 1983).

81. This is not to say that opponents of judicial activism should necessarily completely forswear the use of blunt instruments in Congress. The melancholy fact, they might say, is that human beings who have power rarely consider the possible inappropriateness of having so much power unless they are compelled to do so. Part of the process of "persuading" courts to withdraw their pretensions may be the invocation of otherwise inapt congressional powers to check them—another lesson of Roosevelt's Court-packing attempt.

82. See, for example, Tribe, *Constitutional Choices* (Cambridge: Harvard University Press, 1985), chapt. 5. In *The Constitution, the Courts, and Human Rights* (New Haven: Yale University Press, 1982), Michael Perry is a notable exception in this regard.

83. *Charles River Bride* v. *Warren Bridge,* 11 Peters 420 (1837); *Ogden* v. *Saunders,* 12 Wheaton 213 (1827); *New York* v. *Miln,* 11 Peters 102 (1837); *Cooley* v. *Board of Wardens,* 12 Howard 299 (1852).

84. *Miller* v. *California,* 413 U.S. 15; *Paris Adult Theatre* v. *Slaton,* 413 U.S. 49 (1973).

85. 426 U.S. 833 (1976); *Usery* was overruled in *Garcia* v. *San Antonio MTA,* 469 U.S. 528 (1985).

86. For example, *Harris* v. *New York*, 401 U.S. 222 (1971); *Stone* v. *Powell*, 428 U.S. 465 (1976). "Nibbles" became larger "chunks" in *United States* v. *Leon*, 468 U.S. 897 (1984) and *New York* v. *Quarles*, 467 U.S. 649 (1984).
87. For example, *San Antonio* v. *Rodriguez*, 411 U.S. 1 (1973).
88. *Roe* v. *Wade*, 410 U.S. 113 (1973); *Frontiero* v. *Richardson*, 411 U.S. 677 (1973); *Graham* v. *Richardson*, 403 U.S. 365 (1971).
89. In free speech, compare *Virginia Pharmacy Board* v. *Virginia Consumer Council*, 425 U.S. 748 (1976), and *Nebraska* v. *Stuart*, 427 U.S. 539 (1976), with *Miller* v. *California*, 413 U.S. 15 (1973), and *Branzburg* v. *Hayes*, 408 U.S. 665 (1972). In religion, compare *Committee for Public Education* v. *Nyquist*, 413 U.S. 756 (1973), with *Committee for Public Education* v. *Regan*, 444 U.S. 646 (1980), and *Mueller* v. *Allen*, 463 U.S. 388 (1983). On busing, compare *Swann* v. *Charlotte-Mecklenberg*, 402 U.S. 1 (1971), with *Milliken* v. *Bradley*, 418 U.S. 717 (1974).
90. That *Roe* v. *Wade* may be its most memorable case is certainly ironic, given that the Burger Court consisted mostly of justices appointed by Republican presidents: President Reagan, Sandra Day O'Connor; President Ford, John P. Stevens; President Nixon, Warren E. Burger, Harry A. Blackmum, Lewis F. Powell, Jr., William H. Rehnquist, and President Eisenhower, William J. Brennan. Only Thurgood Marshall, appointed by President Johnson, and Byron White, appointed by President Kennedy, were nominated by Democrats, although all but O'Connor were confirmed by Democratic Senates.

The similarity between the Taney and Burger courts in their tendency to be "conservative" of precedent is noted in Shapiro, "The Supreme Court," p. 203, n. 64.
91. *West Virginia Board of Education* v. *Barnette*, 319 U.S. 624 (1943).
92. In re Griffiths, 413 U.S. 717 (1973).
93. *Weinberger* v. *Wiesenfeld*, 420 U.S. 636 (1975).
94. The Court has contributed to this by its willingness to protect material at the "outer limits of tolerance" according to "contemporary community standards." But if material at the margin is consistently tolerated, those margins will tend constantly to expand. See Clor, *Obscenity and Public Morality* (Chicago: University of Chicago Press, 1969), pp. 55–60.
95. *Adkins* v. *Children's Hospital*, 261 U.S. 525 (1923).
96. *Keyes* v. *Denver School District*, 413 U.S. 921 (1973); see also Graglia, *Disaster by Decree*, chapts. 7–10. The well-known activities of Judge Arthur Garrity in Boston are another example.
97. *Reynolds* v. *Sims*, 377 U.S. 533 (1964).

98. For example, *Hamilton* v. *Schiro*, 338 F. Supp. 1016 (E.D. La. 1970); and *Hodge* v. *Dodd*, 1 Prison L. Rptr. 263 (N.D. Ga. 1972).
99. For example, *Wyatt* v. *Stickney*, 325 F. Supp. 781 (M.D. Ala. 1971), 334 F. Supp. 341 (1971), 344 F. Supp. 373 (1972), 344 F. Supp. 387 (1972).
100. *Serrano* v. *Priest*, 96 Calif. Rptr. 601; *San Antonio* v. *Rodriquez*, 411 U.S. 1 (1973); *Robinson* v. *Cahill*, 62 N.J. 473 (1973).
101. *Miranda* v. *Arizona*, 384 U.S. 436 (1966).
102. 410 U.S. 113 (1973).
103. On the high level of personal integrity of Supreme Court appointees, see Scigliano, *The Supreme Court and the Presidency*, p. 106.
104. Horowitz, *The Courts and Social Policy*, p. 280.
105. 349 U.S. 294 (1955).
106. *Stone* v. *Powell*, 428 U.S. 465 (1976), *United States* v. *Leon*, 468 U.S. 897 (1984).
107. *Memoirs* v. *Massachusetts*, 383 U.S. 413 (1966), overturned by *Miller* v. *California*, 413 U.S. 15 (1973). Strictly speaking, the controlling opinion in *Memoirs* was a plurality opinion and not authoritative in the sense that it could be "overturned"—but that was the practical effect.
108. *Minersville School District* v. *Gobitis*, 310 U.S. 586 (1940).

Chapter Four

1. *Harvard Law Review* 7 (1893): 129; Kurland, ed., *John Marshall* (Chicago: University of Chicago Press, 1967).
2. Ibid., p. 83.
3. Ibid., p. 84.
4. Ibid., pp. 85–86.
5. Ibid., p. 86.
6. Ibid., p. 86.
7. See his comments on the importance of maintaining a strong judiciary in *Democracy in America*, vol. II, (New York: Random House, Vintage, 1945), book IV, chapt. 7, p. 343.
8. Ibid., book II, chapt. 2, p. 104.
9. Ibid., book II, chapt. 10, pp. 136–138.
10. Ibid., book IV, chapt. 6, p. 336.
11. Ibid., book IV, chapt. 6, p. 337.
12. Ibid., book II, chapts. 4, 8, pp. 109–113, 129–132 (quotation at p. 112).
13. Ibid., p. 110.
14. Ibid., vol. I, chapt. 14, pp. 260, 261, 262.

15. Ibid., vol. II, book II, chapt. 4, p. 112.
16. Ibid., book IV, chapt. 7, p. 347.
17. Lincoln, "Message to Congress in Special Session" (July 4, 1861), in *The Writings of Lincoln*, ed. Lapsley (New York: Lamb Publishing Co., 1906), vol. V, p. 337.
18. Cf. *Federalist*, No. 84, p. 438.
19. *Democracy in America* vol. II, appendix BB, p. 388.
20. Ibid., book II, chapt. 4, p. 110; see also vol. I, chapt. 8, p. 165–171.
21. That is, the decline of traditional or constitutional federalism, in which a broad range of political issues had their ultimate resolution at the state or local level and were not subject to review by the national government. Debate about federalism continues, of course, but it is a different debate, about whether Congress should use its undoubted constitutional power in a given area or exercise its discretion to leave such matters to the states. This is a policy, not a constitutional, question.
22. Sandalow, "Constitutional Interpretation," *Michigan Law Review* 79 (1981): 1033, 1042.
23. See Jaffa, "The Nature and Origin of the American Party System," in *Political Parties, U.S.A.*, ed. Goldwin (Chicago: Rand McNally, 1961).
24. Nelson Polsby makes a similar argument about "great presidents" in "Against Presidential Greatness," *Commentary* 63 (January, 1977): 61–64.
25. Mayhew, *Congress: The Electoral Connection* (New Haven: Yale University Press, 1974). Mayhew suggests that representatives act to get reelected, and to the extent that this motivation is dominant (even if Mayhew overstates it somewhat), one must doubt whether they would have strong incentives to deal carefully with constitutional issues.
26. *Nixon v. Herndon*, 273 U.S. 536 (1927); *Nixon v. Condon*, 286 U.S. 73 (1932); *Smith v. Allwright*, 321 U.S. 649 (1944); *Terry v. Adams*, 345 U.S. 461 (1953); *Yates v. United States*, 354 U.S. 298 (1957); *Scales v. United States*, 367 U.S. 203 (1961); *Tinker v. DesMoines*, 393 U.S. 503 (1969).
27. See Baum, *The Supreme Court* (Washington, D.C.: Congressional Quarterly, 1981), p. 212; Scheingold, *The Politics of Rights* (New Haven: Yale University Press, 1974), chapt. 9 (although Scheingold emphasizes the positive aspect—the deliberate use of the courts to mobilize groups—rather than the negative aspect—the inadvertent mobilization of groups by decisions they dislike).

28. Letter to Thomas Jefferson October 17, 1788, in *The Writings of James Madison*, ed. Hunt (New York: G. P. Putnam's Sons, 1900–1910), vol. V, p. 273.

29. Choper, *Judicial Review and the National Political Process: A Functional Reconsideration of the Role of the Supreme Court* (Chicago: University of Chicago Press, 1980), pp. 92–93.

30. On American political culture, see Devine, *The Political Culture of the United States* (Boston: Little, Brown, 1972).

31. Rostow, "The Democratic Character of Judicial Review," *Harvard Law Review* 66 (1952): 193, 210.

32. *McCulloch* v. *Maryland*, 4 Wheaton 316, 423 (1819).

33. Cf. Devine, *The Political Culture of the United States*, pp. 265ff.

34. *New State Ice Co.* v. *Liebmann*, 285 U.S. 262, 311 (1932).

35. This is not to deny that it is essential for the judiciary to protect clear constitutional rights, which are often essential to guarantee access to the political process. Denial of voting rights on racial grounds, for instance, is a clear constitutional violation. Even in this area, however, one might argue that democratic tendencies would lead to vindication of such rights through the ordinary political process in the long run, although perhaps it would be an unjustifiably long run.

36. Note that judicial activists who are quick to dismiss federalism on the grounds that it is outdated, and that there is a popular tacit consent to its substantial modification, would dismiss out of hand the legitimacy of that kind of argument applied to civil liberties. If judicial activists can not win many battles in the legislature, their popular support is quite weak and perhaps there is popular "tacit consent" to modifications of the constitutional principles they seek to protect. They might rightly criticize such alleged tacit consent on the grounds that it was not the result of reflective deliberation on the principles, but merely a tangential effect of immediate policy preferences. The same argument, however, is applicable to any supposed tacit consent to the modification of federalism.

37. After all, judicial activists very readily assert the satisfactory character of legislative determinations on most policy questions, especially regarding economic matters since 1937. They need not agree with particular results, but they are satisfied enough to have the legislature rather than the judiciary calling the shots on these many matters. While since 1937 liberals have typically assumed a double standard—judicial activism in civil liberties, extreme judicial restraint, indeed abdication, in economic matters, except for egalitarian aspects of social welfare legis-

lation—this double standard has not been successfully defended against a critique such as Robert McCloskey's "Economic Due Process: An Exhumation and Re-burial," *Supreme Court Review* 34 (1962), where the reburial is performed on much less persuasive grounds than the exhumation. This problem has led to some emerging "property rights activism," which liberals are usually less than enthusiastic about. See, for example, Richard A. Epstein, *Takings: Private Property and the Power of Eminent Domain* (Cambridge: Harvard University Press, 1985) and Stephen Macedo, *The New Right* v. *the Constitution* (Washington, D.C.: Cato Institute, 1986).

38. It might be argued that modern judicial power does not preclude legislative activity, such as defending freedom of speech in the first instance before the issues get to court. As a practical matter, however, that an issue will eventually be resolved elsewhere undermines any incentive to deal with it: Why use up the scarce and precious legislative time on matters where some other institution has the final say?

39. Sullivan, Piereson, and Marcus, *Political Tolerance and American Democracy* (Chicago: University of Chicago Press, 1982), pp. 175–186.

40. McCloskey, "Economic Due Process," n. 37.

41. 448 U.S. 297 (1980).

42. This alienation might have taken the form of "dropping out of the political system," or the more dangerous form of outside radical action, such as bombing abortion clinics. Warren Court decisions certainly contributed to the phenomenon of alienation among those who formed the core of support for Alabama governor George Wallace in his bid for the presidency in 1968.

43. On the First Amendment, see Berns, *The First Amendment and the Future of American Democracy* (New York: Basic Books, 1976); and on reapportionment, see Raoul Berger, *Government by Judiciary: The Transformation of the Fourteenth Amendment* (Cambridge: Harvard University Press, 1976) chapt. 5, and Justice Harlan's dissenting opinions in the reapportionment decisions, such as *Reynolds* v. *Sims*.

Chapter Five

1. The best-known example of a *Carolene Products* approach is Ely, *Democracy and Distrust: A Theory of Judicial Review* (Cambridge: Harvard University Press, 1980). His rationale for protecting minority rights is different from the one described in the text, however.

2. This view is partly expressed by the notion of a "colloquy" between Court and legislature described by Alexander Bickel in *The Least Dangerous Branch* (Indianapolis: Bobbs-Merrill, 1962), p. 156.

3. Cf. Lusky, *By What Right? A Commentary on the Supreme Court's Power to Revise the Constitution* (Charlotteville, Va.: Michie Press, 1975).

4. Ely makes a similar suggestion in *Democracy and Distrust*, when he says that laws based on old stereotypes regarding formerly politically powerless disadvantaged groups, such as women, should be struck down but then upheld if they are passed again, now that women are no longer politically powerless.

5. For a broad view of the *Carolene Products* footnote, see Lusky, *By What Right?* chapts. 6 and 7.

6. Ely's *Democracy and Distrust* is often considered a defense of a more limited form of modern judicial review, based on the *Carolene Products* footnote. On analysis, however, his theory can be used to justify even cases that he strongly attacked himself. See the use of his theory to justify *Roe* v. *Wade* (of which Ely is a strong critic) in a review by Archibald Cox in *Harvard Law Review* 94 (1981): 700.

7. For a *reductio ad absurdum* of what the First Amendment protects, especially in conjunction with the overbreadth doctrine, see the facts of *California* v. *LaRue*, 409 U.S. 109 (1972), described in Justice Rehnquist's opinion for the Court.

8. For a survey of the leading theories of judicial review, with incisive criticisms of many of them, from a viewpoint altogether different from mine, see Tushnet, *Red, White, and Blue: A Critical Analysis of Constitutional Law* (Cambridge: Harvard University Press, 1988), part I.

9. Letter from Thomas Jefferson to James Madison, September 6, 1789, in *The Writings of Thomas Jefferson*, ed. Washington (Philadelphia: Lippincott, 1869), vol. III, pp. 102–109. There is an echo of Jefferson in Ely's critical remarks about the dead ruling the living in *Democracy and Distrust*, chapt. 2.

10. This scenario is unlikely because even one or two judges who preferred to see the law simply dead could probably negotiate such a statement out of most Court opinions. Moreover, it would be extremely awkward to tell the immediate litigant "you lose," while promising that future litigants will win under the same law if it is repassed by the legislature.

11. Diamond, "Ethics and Politics: The American Way," in *The Moral Foundations of the American Republic*, ed. Horowitz (Charlottesville, Va.: University of Virginia Press, 1977), especially sect. iv.

12. Cf. Storing, "The Constitution and the Bill of Rights" in *Taking the Constitution Seriously*, ed. McDowell (Dubuque: Kendall/Hunt, 1981), p. 279; Kendall and Carey, *The Basic Symbols of the American Political Tradition* (Baton Rouge: Louisiana State University Press, 1970), chapt. 7. Note also that James Madison, in a letter to Thomas Jefferson on October 17, 1789, discussing the merits of a bill of rights, includes the judicial enforcement of a bill of rights as an "additional" favorable argument, almost an afterthought.

13. *Federalist*, No. 81 (Wills ed., p. 411).

14. Cf. Kristol, "The American Judicial Power and the American Regime" (Ph.D. diss., Harvard University, 1979).

15. This is not to suggest that there was universal agreement about judicial review in the founding. Note, however, that the major source of attacks on the mainstream position (i.e., Jeffersonians) would have minimized the "public law" functions of the courts even more.

16. On standing, see Kristol, "The American Judicial Power", n. 11; and on remedial powers, see McDowell, *Equity and the Constitution* (Chicago: University of Chicago Press, 1982).

17. I think Michael Perry's ready acceptance of political control of the Court by means of congressional control of the Court's appellate jurisdiction would fall into this category. See *The Constitution, the Courts, and Human Rights* (New Haven: Yale University Press, 1982).

18. Cardozo, *The Nature of the Judicial Process* (New Haven: Yale University Press, 1921), p. 79.

19. For an interesting view of the legal landscape as it appeared to the young Holmes, see his *Collected Legal Papers* (New York: Harcourt Brace & Howe, 1920), pp. 301–302.

20. See his letter to Haynes (February 25, 1831) in Hunt, *The Writings of James Madison* (G. P. Putnam's Sons, 1900–1910), vol. IX, pp. 442–443.

21. On the foundation of judicial review in such popular perceptions, see Bork, "Neutral Principles and Some First Amendment Problems," *Indiana Law Journal* 47 (1971): 1, 3–4. An example of the power of older notions of the judicial role is found in the fact that, despite the politicization of recent hearings on Supreme Court nominations, most Americans would still be offended if they heard a Senate Judiciary Committee member say, "I will not vote for you unless you commit yourself to vote this way on a future case," despite efforts from pressure groups to secure just such commitments.

SELECTED BIBLIOGRAPHY

Abraham, Henry. *The Judicial Process*. 5th ed. New York: Oxford University Press, 1986.

Ackerman, Bruce. "Discovering the Constitution." *Yale Law Journal* 93 (1984): 1013.

Agresto, John. *The Supreme Court and Constitutional Democracy*. Ithaca, N.Y.: Cornell University Press, 1987.

Barber, Sotirios. *On What the Constitution Means*. Baltimore, Md.: Johns Hopkins University Press, 1984.

Baum, Lawrence. *The Supreme Court*. Washington, D.C.: Congressional Quarterly, 1981.

Berger, Raoul. *Government by Judiciary: The Transformation of the Fourteenth Amendment*. Cambridge: Harvard University Press, 1976.

Berns, Walter. *The First Amendment and the Future of American Democracy*. New York: Basic Books, 1976.

———."Judicial Review and the Rights and Laws of Nature." In *In Defense of Liberal Democracy*. Chicago: Gateway Editions, 1984.

Bickel, Alexander. *The Least Dangerous Branch*. Indianapolis: Bobbs-Merrill, 1962.

———. *The Morality of Consent*. New Haven: Yale University Press, 1975.

Blasi, Vincent, ed. *The Burger Court: The Counterrevolution That Wasn't*. New Haven: Yale University Press, 1983.

Bond, James E. *The Art of Judging*. New Brunswick, N.J.: Transaction Books, 1987.

Bork, Robert. "Neutral Principles and Some First Amendment Problems." *Indiana Law Journal* 47 (1971): 1.

———. *The Tempting of America*. New York: Free Press, 1990.

Bradley, Gerard V. *Church-State Relationships in America*. New York: Greenwood Press, 1987.

Brest, Paul. *Processes of Constitutional Decisionmaking*. Boston: Little, Brown, 1975.

Cardozo, Benjamin. *The Nature of the Judicial Process*. New Haven: Yale University Press, 1921.

Carter, Lief. *Contemporary Constitutional Lawmaking: The Supreme Court and the Art of Politics*. New York: Pergamon Press, 1985.

Cavanaugh, Ralph, and Austin Sarat. "Thinking About Courts: Toward and Beyond a Jurisprudence of Judicial Competence." *Law and Society Review* 14 (1979–80): 371.

Chayes, Abram. "The Role of the Judge in Public Law Litigation." *Harvard Law Review* 89 (1976): 1281.

Choper, Jesse. *Judicial Review and the National Political Process: A Functional Reconsideration of the Role of the Supreme Court*. Chicago: University of Chicago Press, 1980.

Clinton, Robert. *Marbury v. Madison and Judicial Review*. Lawrence: University of Kansas Press, 1989.

Cord, Robert. *Separation of Church and State: Historical Fact and Current Fiction*. New York: Lambeth Press, 1982.

Cox, Archibald. *The Role of the Supreme Court in American Government*. New York: Oxford University Press, 1976.

Currie, David P. *The Constitution in the Supreme Court: The First Hundred Years, 1789–1888*. Chicago: University of Chicago Press, 1985.

Curtis, Michael Kent. *No State Shall Abridge: The Fourteenth Amendment and the Bill of Rights*. Durham, N.C.: Duke University Press, 1986.

Dworkin, Ronald. *Taking Rights Seriously*. Cambridge: Harvard University Press, 1977.

———. *Law's Empire*. Cambridge: Harvard University Press, 1986.

Elliott, Ward. *The Rise of Guardian Democracy*. Cambridge: Harvard University Press, 1974.

Ely, John Hart. *Democracy and Distrust: A Theory of Judicial Review*. Cambridge: Harvard University Press, 1980.

Epstein, Richard A. *Takings: Private Property and the Power of Eminent Domain*. Cambridge: Harvard University Press, 1985.

Fiss, Owen. "The Forms of Justice." *Harvard Law Review* 93 (1979): 1.

Fleming, Macklin. *The Price of Perfect Justice*. New York: Basic Books, 1974.

Gangi, William. "Judicial Expansionism: An Evaluation of the Ongoing Debate." *Ohio Northern University Law Review* 8 (1981): 1.

Graglia, Lino A. *Disaster By Decree: The Supreme Court Decisions on Race and the Schools*. Ithaca, N.Y.: Cornell University Press, 1976.

Grey, Thomas. "Do We Have an Unwritten Constitution?" *Stanford Law Review* 27 (1975): 703.

Halpern, Stephen, and Charles Lamb. *Supreme Court Activism and Restraint*. Lexington, Mass.: Lexington Books, 1982.

Hastings Constitutional Law Quarterly 6, no. 2 (Winter 1979). Symposium on Raoul Berger's *Government by Judiciary*.

Horowitz, Donald. *The Courts and Social Policy*. Washington, D.C.: Brookings, 1977.

Jacobsohn, Gary. *The Supreme Court and the Decline of Constitutional Aspiration*. Totowa, N.J.: Rowman & Littlefield, 1986.

Lasser, William. *The Limits of Judicial Power: The Supreme Court in American Politics*. Chapel Hill, N.C.: University of North Carolina Press, 1988.

Levinson, Sanford. *Constitutional Faith*. Princeton: Princeton University Press, 1988.

Levy, Leonard. *Legacy of Suppression*. Cambridge: Harvard University Press, 1960.

———. *Original Intent and the Framers' Constitution*. New York: Macmillan, 1988.

Lusky, Louis. *By What Right?: A Commentary on the Supreme Court's Power to Revise the Constitution*. Charlottesville, Va.: The Michie Co., 1975.

Macedo, Stephen. *The New Right v. the Constitution*. Washington, D.C.: Cato Institute, 1986.

McCloskey, Robert. *The American Supreme Court*. Chicago: University of Chicago Press, 1960.

McDowell, Gary. *Equity and the Constitution*. Chicago: University of Chicago Press, 1982.

————. *Curbing the Courts: The Constitution and the Limits of Judicial Power.* Baton Rouge: Louisiana State University Press, 1988.

Miller, Arthur Sellwyn. *Toward Increased Judicial Activism: The Political Role of the Supreme Court.* Westport, Conn.: Greenwood Press, 1982.

Monaghan, Henry. "Constitutional Adjudication: The When and Who." *Yale Law Journal* 82 (1973): 1363.

Morgan, Richard E. *Disabling America: The "Rights Industry" in Our Time.* New York: Basic Books, 1984.

Neely, Richard. *How Courts Govern America.* New Haven: Yale University Press, 1981.

Ohio State Law Journal 42, no. 1 (1981). Symposium on Judicial Review Versus Democracy.

Perry, Michael. *The Constitution, the Courts, and Human Rights.* New Haven: Yale University Press, 1982.

————. *Morality, Politics, and Law.* New York: Oxford University Press, 1988.

Rabkin, Jeremy. *Judicial Compulsions: How Public Law Distorts Public Policy.* New York: Basic Books, 1989.

Rostow, Eugene. "The Democratic Character of Judicial Review." *Harvard Law Review* 66 (1953): 193.

Sandalow, Terrance. "Constitutional Interpretation." *Michigan Law Review* 79 (1981): 1033.

Scigliano, Robert. *The Supreme Court and the Presidency.* New York: Free Press, 1971.

Shapiro, Martin. "The Supreme Court: From Warren to Burger." In *The New American Political System,* edited by King. Washington, D.C.: American Enterprise Institute, 1978.

Smith, Rogers M. *Liberalism and American Constitutional Law.* Cambridge: Harvard University Press, 1985.

Southern California Law Review 58, nos. 1 and 2 (January 1985). Symposium on Interpretation.

Thayer, James Bradley. "The Origin and Scope of the American Doctrine of Constitutional Law." *Harvard Law Review* 7 (1893): 129.

Theberge, Leonard. *The Judiciary in a Democratic Society.* Lexington, Mass.: Lexington Books, 1977.

Tocqueville, Alexis de. *Democracy in America.* New York: Random House, Vintage, 1945.

Tribe, Laurence. *Constitutional Choices.* Cambridge: Harvard University Press, 1985.

————. *God Save This Honorable Court.* New York: Random House, 1985.

Tushnet, Mark. *Red, White, and Blue: A Critical Analysis of Constitutional Law*. Cambridge: Harvard University Press, 1988.

Wellington, Harry. "The Nature of Judicial Review." *Yale Law Journal* 91 (1982): 487.

Wolfe, Christopher. *The Rise of Modern Judicial Review: From Constitutional Interpretation to Judge-Made Law*. New York: Basic Books, 1986.

Index